DATE DUE

~~JY 14'97~~		
~~MY 25'98~~		
~~		
MY 29'99		

DEMCO 38-296

I strapped on

a sixty-pound pack and walked into

the California desert . . .

Still Wild, Always Wild

A Journey into the Desert Wilderness of California

Susan Zwinger

PHOTOGRAPHS BY JEFF GARTON

SIERRA CLUB BOOKS

SAN FRANCISCO

A TEHABI BOOK

…2 by John Muir, has devoted itself to the study and protection of the earth's …ins, wetlands, woodlands, wild shores and rivers, deserts and plains. The …fers books to the public as a nonprofit educational service in the hope that …ding of the Club's basic concerns. The point of view expressed in each book, however, does not necessarily represent that of the Club. The Sierra Club has some sixty chapters coast to coast, in Canada, Hawaii, and Alaska. For information about how you may participate in its programs to preserve wilderness and the quality of life, please address inquiries to Sierra Club, 85 Second Street, San Francisco, CA 94105.

Library of Congress Cataloging in Publication Data

Zwinger, Susan, 1947-
        Still wild, always wild: a journey into the desert wilderness of California / Susan Zwinger;
photographs by Jeff Garton
        p.   cm.
"A Tehabi Book."
Includes bibliographical references (p.   ) and index.
ISBN 0-87156-886-1 (hbk).—ISBN 0-87156-887-X (pbk)
1. Deserts—California. 2. Deserts—California—Pictorial works. 3. California—Description and travel.
4. California—Pictorial works. I. Title.

F866.2.Z95   1997   96-24201
917.94 ' 0954—dc20   CIP

Still Wild, Always Wild was conceived and produced by Tehabi Books.

Nancy Cash–*Managing Editor*; Susan Wels–*Manuscript Editor*; Anne Hayes–*Copy Editor*; Jeff Campbell–*Copy Proofer*; Ken DellaPenta–*Indexer*; Elden Hughes–*Technical Advisor*; Sam Lewis–*Art Director*; Andy Lewis–*Art Director*; Tom Lewis–*Editorial and Design Director*; Richard Carter–*Map Illustrator*; Sharon Lewis–*Controller*; Chris Capen–*President*. For more information on Tehabi Books call 800-243-7259, or visit us at http://www.tehabi.com

Sierra Club Books and Tehabi Books, in association with The Basic Foundation, a not-for-profit organiza-tion whose primary mission is reforestation, will facilitate the planting of two trees for every one tree used in the manufacture of this book. This edition is printed on acid-free paper that meets the American National Standards Institute z39.48 Standard.

Printed in Hong Kong through Mandarin Offset. First Edition 1996

Page 1: Cadiz dunes in the Sheephole Mountains

Page 2-3: Golden hills in the Coyote Mountains

Page 4: Ocotillo in Anza-Borrego desert

CONTENTS

Somewhere out there is a land grand enough to hold all life's passions and contradictions, to expand one's soul with vast possibilities, to awaken all one's senses.

To find it, search north from the Mexican border up through the California desert via backroads and wilderness areas, through the lost and forgotten and least-explored outback. Find those places least written about. Ask locals. Be adventurous. Expand into infinity in a desert night. Take on the night vision of an elf owl, the radar of a leaf-nosed bat, the ears of a kit fox, the vibration sensors of a Gambel's quail. Turn off the radio. Turn off the stereo. Get out of the vehicle and walk. Gaze at the desert with the eyes of an eagle, then with the eyes of a snake. Sit for long periods of time in silence, listening. After a while, the desert will speak to you.

Time in the great deserts of the West is very different from city time. Because the earth's crust is sliced open, and so many objects from past history lie preserved in the dry, clean air, desert time is like layers of clear plate glass. You can drop down through them, intersecting lives separated by centuries. In the desert, antiquity is interlayered with the present—as when ancient rock art lies within military testing grounds. Sitting near a wall painted with a giant shaman figure created two thousand years ago, you may think you hear a foot thud on the hardpacked desert floor and turn swiftly to see no one. You may imagine the shaman dressing as, then actually becoming, a god in order to call the rain. You may hear the ladder creak as he emerges from a sacred cave, having performed a healing ritual.

Or you may hear the hoof beats of a seventeenth-century padre gingerly riding from one hardship to the next, seeking native people to convert, inserting Old World Spanish saints into the native pantheon.

Or you may overhear a voice from a century ago, an old white prospector having a talk with his mule,

Desert holly, whose silvery leaves are coated with salt exuded from the plant, contrasts dramatically with lava flows throughout the desert.

With the Eyes of an Eagle

THE CALIFORNIA DESERT PROTECTION ACT

demanding from the desert too much, too soon, and too easy.

Simultaneously, you may hear contemporary Chemehuevi people chanting clan songs that will continue their tradition down through the ages, or hear a researcher mumbling at his Global Positioning Satellite navigator as he tracks desert tortoise.

In the desert, you will meet animals possessed with people-wisdom. You will glimpse Coyote, the Trickster, darting in and out, through the edge of cities, sewing an urban civilization uneasily onto the desert. The daredevil jackrabbit will dash two inches in front of your car bumper, making bets with his cronies about how close he can come to death. He will always win. The horned lizard, all pimpled and lumpy, will lie passively in your hand, too stuffed with sun and insects to object.

In your imagination, you will find yourself conducting interviews with the men who hunted with *atl-atl* twenty-six thousand years ago over near Barstow. You will find yourself chattering across time, across language, and across cultural gaps with the Ancient Ones as if they stood in your kitchen. Which, at your campfire, they will. They will teach you the rich variety of uses for the plants and animals. You will find your sensory perception far lacking compared to their own. Yet the longer you remain in wild places and outside your vehicle, the more your hearing, smelling, touching, electromagnetic radar, and vibration sensors will return to you.

Nowhere else on earth is geologic time so exposed as in a desert. There, you will travel swiftly through geological eras as you pass through highly eroded mountains, bizarre volcanic necks and cones, endless salt playas, and towering sand dunes in sensuous curves of pink and tan. You will pass through brick red and black dorsal fins jutting eight hundred feet up out of the earth as if stegosaurs cavorted just under the ground, past long black snakes of glassy lava one hundred feet high, through badlands as colorful as an artist's palette, through narrow, contorted canyons, through limestone caverns, and through the world's largest Joshua tree forest. Each profusely flowering cactus, each hidden desert waterfall and plunge pool, will open senses you barely knew you had.

* * *

The fragile California desert stretches 100 miles from east to west and 240 miles from north to south. For ten long years, hundreds of American citizens worked to protect its remarkable wild lands, which include three of the great deserts of the world—the Mojave, the lower tip of the Great Basin, and the northern wedge of the Sonoran. On October 31, 1994, President Clinton signed the California Desert Protection Act into law, protecting another 3.57 million acres of land as wilderness. The sixty-nine new wilderness areas are as different from one another as topography can be—from high alpine snow fields discharging roaring streams to dry, barren salt playas—and they will take a lifetime to explore.

The Desert Protection Act created two new national parks, Death Valley and Joshua Tree. At over 3.3 million acres, Death Valley is now the largest park in the lower forty-eight states. Joshua Tree was increased to 793,000 acres by including natural ecosystems which had previously extended beyond the former monument boundaries. The act also established the dramatic landscape between Interstates 15 and 40 as the Mojave National Preserve, the newest addition to the National Park Service. In addition, wilderness habitat adjacent to Anza-Borrego and Red Rock Canyon State Parks has been greatly expanded.

Despite the passage of the act, debate continues as ferociously as ever: Why save so much desert? We have long disparaged it as "wasteland," "barren," "badland," "bleak," and "evil." Early writers and explorers claimed that it was unlivable, undesirable, unprofitable, and that every organism in it was at war with every other. Among European white explorers, the desert provoked feelings of anxiety and hopelessness. They expected to be attacked by fang, claw, and thorn

Names hold power. And we have named the desert wilderness Death Valley, the Devil's Playground, Skull Valley, Last Chance Mountains, and the Badlands. In naming, we shape the wisdom of future generations. Nowhere are our land-use ethics and symbolic understanding of the desert more clearly revealed than in our naming process of desert phenomena. As in war, we devalue our "enemies" so that we can slaughter them with a clean conscience.

In the same manner, those who would like the "freedom" to continue to destroy the desert have been disseminating a dangerous and calculated pack of lies through newspapers, talk shows, and cyberspace. Here are a few:

1. All the roads to the new wilderness areas are closed. (Truth: Thousands of miles of road remain open, and "cherry stems" into wilderness areas provide access.)

2. Only rich, elite environmentalists can enjoy the desert because they can afford to be dropped in by helicopter. (Truth: The desert, except for military ranges and small research areas, is open to all citizens and is one of the cheapest forms of entertainment available. Citizens who care about the environment come from all walks of life and all income levels.)

3. The federal government is destroying your freedom. (Truth: Federal and state environmental protection laws reflect the wishes of a majority of citizens to preserve valuable life forms and topography for future generations.)

4. The California Desert Protection Act and related laws are un-American. (Truth: One of the greatest inventions that Americans have offered the world is our wilderness and park systems and our other efforts to protect the shrinking, remaining wild places on earth.)

We need the Desert Protection Act because the California desert environment is in grave danger—a fact that is supported by research in many branches of science: geology, botany, biology, chemistry, meteorology, sociology, and anthropology to name a few. In California and across the globe, man has been stripping the desert of vegetation through grazing, mining, gravel pits, ever-expanding off-road-vehicle

Still Wild, Always Wild

trails, and an unsustainable increase in human population. Moreover, the California desert's proximity to some of the world's largest and fastest-growing urban areas—Los Angeles and Las Vegas—causes the fragile balances of nature to be overwhelmed by modern vehicles, roadways, resource extraction, housing expansion, and recreation. Finite fossil groundwater is recklessly depleted by golf courses and elegant resort expansions at the expense of the very ecosystem that attracts the growing population. For instance, in spite of the fact that the groundwater beneath Anza-Borrego State Park is sinking by two feet a year, the valley of Borrego Springs continues to build swimming pools, golf courses, and elaborate resorts, and agriculture continues to increase.

The loss of desert wilderness has serious consequences for all of us. Humans have much to learn from observing life at the critical edge of survival: its marvelous adaptations to blowing sand, high altitude, or extreme heat may someday prove invaluable to humans. For instance, within the volatile oils which protect desert plants from dessication, we have found many blessings for mankind, from the medicinal to the mechanical. The California desert also supports many plant and animal species that live nowhere else on earth. These species have evolved unique strategies to survive in extreme conditions, and within their DNA strands may be keys that can help us adapt to extremely limited resources. For example, we already know that the genes of a humble dune grass can revitalize our cereal grain species. Because we grow in giant monocultures, the grains we now depend on are subject to waves of disease, such as the fungus that destroyed Ireland's potatoes in the nineteenth century.

Yet we cannot claim that the only reason desert species should be saved is their useful-ness to mankind. We must assume that each one is absolutely necessary in its own being. Our humanity depends on the farsighted act of saving the unique life forms of the desert, life forms which occur nowhere else on the planet. Complete natural phenomena such as bird and butterfly migrations are currently being destroyed because the wilderness links between South, Central, and North America are broken. When we lose one songbird or one butterfly species, we lose part of ourselves.

Desert wilderness is our American heritage. By protecting it, we give a gift not only to our nation but to the entire world. It increases our self-worth as a country and is a sign of our security and wisdom. It speaks well of us as a society that we are wealthy enough in both spiritual and natural resources that we can choose to stop before we destroy the legacy of our remaining wild lands.

* * *

I sit now on this stone shelf scribbling into my notebook, watching light drain from the landscape. A bat jerks by in flight, a tiny speck, squeaking like an unoiled valve. Elf owls draw silken flight vectors across the sky, and Gambel's quail cross so close to my foot that their claws are audible. Coyotes begin mad chattering on cliffs like human babies crying.

The sky deepens to cobalt, then to eggplant. Cliffs sponge into black. Black clumps of rabbit brush appear to float above the desert floor. Something large and catlike ripples by on silent paws. Time in the desert is so fluid that it seems to flow backward as well as forward, carrying me along.

Even the steepest volcanic slopes of the Last Chance Mountains support a healthy ecosystem of shrubs and animal life.

I gaze out from Carrizo Gorge Overlook above Interstate 8 and piece together the new Sonoran wilderness where I will hike and backpack over the next two weeks. On foot, I will cover sixty miles of the pristine yet long-traveled desert sands. It's the edges and borders and ecotones that drive me wild. I need to know how the Mexican Sonoran melts into the United States' Sonoran, how the Peninsular Mountains of coastal California melt into the Sonoran Desert floor, and how Anza-Borrego State Park flows into its adjacent wild lands: Carrizo Gorge Wilderness, 15,700 acres of deep canyons; the Jacumba Wilderness, 33,670 acres of rugged waterless mountains; and the Coyote Mountains, 17,000 acres of outrageously colored rock.

Far to the north, the cobalt ridge of the Santa Rosa Mountains entices me to backpack deep into an ancient Cahuilla village in Rockhouse Canyon. Closer to me stand the Fish Creek Mountains, full of pure gypsum, and the Coyote Mountains, with their sediments of a six-million-year-old sea. In between, the Carrizo Badlands: I ache to explore their four-hundred-foot cones of gold, red, green, and purple remnants of marine reefs, lake deposits, and ancient Colorado River deltas. Within the Badlands, I will tromp along with mastodons, early llamas, horses, tapirs, and saber-toothed tigers, or hang with giant sloths—twenty thousand years too late.

The Sonoran Desert is the youngest North American desert, having existed for only the last twelve thousand years. It stretches from 23 degrees north in Baja California, Mexico, to 35 degrees north on the border with Arizona. Mostly lying in Mexico, it spills over the US border with its lush variety of bizarre life forms—twenty-foot-tall cacti, raucous carrion-eating birds, wily reptiles, and plants endemic only to the southernmost edge of the United States. As a subtropical desert, it tends to have a greater number of species than do the more temperate desert habitats.

Climbing up Bow Willow Canyon means threading through thick carrizo reeds and under California fan palms.

Overlooking Carrizo Gorge
UP BOW WILLOW CANYON FROM THE DESERT FLOOR

I have driven fifteen hundred miles from my rainy home in Washington State, longing for the Sonoran's magic—life forms and weather distinctly different from those found in any other desert. Here, the unique pattern of rainfall creates the largest cactus in the world—the saguaro, strange trees with green bark; the palo verde; and bizarre forms of the lily family, the yucca and nolina. Long, gentle winter rains from the coast and the shorter, more intense summer rains from the southeast make possible the outlandish ocotillo, the eight-foot-high teddy bear cholla, the fragrant desert lavender shrub, and the elephant tree with its water-swelled, rhinoceros-skinned trunk and lemon-smelling leaves.

I throw my worn-out army poncho, Therm-a-Rest mattress, and twenty-seven-year-old sleeping bag on the sandy, dry ground because I want to wake with the breath of the Sonoran in my nostrils. In the damp morning or after rain, odors of incredible intensity emanate from desert plants that have evolved volatile oils to prevent desiccation: vivid lemons, pungent pines, lavender, mint, sage, rosemary, creosote, and intoxicating earth smells.

It is early February, and Carrizo Gorge Overlook is an ideal place for my exploration to begin. Below me, dropping three thousand feet down, the In-ko-pah, Carrizo, and Bow Willow Gorges look like arid crevices of rock boulders. I know that a hike up from the bottom of Bow Willow will reveal hidden palm oases, waterfalls, and cool pools after a rain, yet because of this barren view, I don't believe it yet. This overlook straddles the transition between the peninsular zone's moist mountain climate and the dramatic Sonoran Desert. I stand at the serrated-knife-edge of two ecosystems and their exceptionally rich variety of species. Last night I slept half a mile back from this escarpment under lush old madronas, huge manzanitas with thick trunks, and deep green oak trees. Yet here, the lush foliage of ocean cliffs dovetails with the scrub of desert floor: *Ephedra viridis* (bright green Mormon tea), desert scrub oak, rabbit brush, sage, and oval-leaved buckwheat. Nuttal's woodpecker, scrub jay, and chickadee of the mountain chaparral mix air waves with Cooper's hawk, turkey vulture, and a magnificent eagle with a flashing golden head.

To the east-northeast, the whiter-than-white Salton Sea shimmers below sea level. Far to the southeast, Picacho Peak Wilderness drops toward the Colorado River; I plan to go there next. To the southeast, the Mexican border's steep mountain terrain, the Jacumba Wilderness, sinks from high

Standing on Carrizo Gorge Overlook, I can see clear north to the Santa Rosa Mountains, far east toward Picacho Peak, and south to Jacumba on the Mexican border.

Although badlands may
appear lifeless from above,
smoke trees, which grow in the
arroyo, harbor entire life
systems.

coastal mountains on the west to sea level in a matter of miles. The US Border Patrol sits outside the waterless wilderness and waits for thirsty illegal aliens.

Directly below me is the infamous Carrizo Corridor. I stare at this barren—or so it seems from up here—desert strip, which was an obvious route for Native Americans traveling by foot between the interior and the coast. Because they knew how to listen to the desert, what to eat, where to look for water, and sought the guidance of shamans, the ancestors of the Cahuilla would pass through with relative ease, taking notice of the great beauty around them.

Beauty, however, was not the preoccupation of the first Europeans who passed through this rugged, "impenetrable" topography. Here, where less than an inch of rain per year may fall and the temperature day after day may soar to 108 degrees, thousands of soldiers, miners, settlers, Spanish friars, snake oil peddlers, outlaws, and dreamers crossed this dry expanse, passing from palm grove to palm grove, spring to spring. Their bodies, composed of 92 percent water, would be incapacitated by a 2 percent water loss; at 8 percent loss they were dead. Death from dehydration is awful, slow, and torturous, with swollen tongue and hallucinations.

I imagine each of these Native American and European travelers leaving a different colored ribbon behind them in their wanderings. Then, in my mind's eye, I add the silver cross-hatching of railroad, the powder blues and pale greens of 1950s Chevys along old Route 99, and the strong reds, dark greens, and blacks of sport utility vehicles on State Route 2. Their intersections weave an intricate crochet of hope, intent, and culture.

Many of the threads, however, end abruptly—explorer or pioneer fallen, desiccated hands outreached toward springs, men slumped over fried radiators, miners picked clean by coyotes, ill-prepared pioneers carried off in the guts of vultures. Just so much dried, bleached detritus on the desert pavement.

Bow Willow Gorge to Carrizo Gorge Overlook

Before dawn the next morning, I drive an hour, through the dramatic Jacumba boulders and into the bottom of Bow Willow Gorge in Anza-Borrego State Park. Soon after dawn, there on the Sonoran Desert floor, I look up again to the Carrizo Gorge Overlook where I stood yesterday and have a burning desire to make my way up there on foot—four thousand feet above. I want to know intimately, increment by increment, plant by plant, how such an enormous ecological-altitudinal change unfolds.

At the lower end, Bow Willow Wash begins as a groggy, quarter-mile-wide, deep sand arroyo where creosote and mesquite are half buried in the debris of the last flash flood. Shiny black phainopeplas—cardinal-shaped, obsidian-black birds—start up from their bushes like black holes in the air.

At thirteen hundred feet, the day is heating up: no shade and no sign of water. It is my first day back in the desert. I feel anxious. To take my mind off my hot feet, I notice the bright chartreuse

Ocotillos bloom in the Carrizo Badlands below the distant Fish Creek Mountains.

and red balls of mistletoe beginning to bloom in the dull brown shrubs. Dripping with sweat, miserably hot, I hear a sudden swell of bird chirruping.

One hundred feet below me, the shrub down in the arroyo appears gray in color. Now that I am closer I see its color is bright green. Water! The first surface water has appeared where there has been no water for almost a year. It has instantly created a stream habitat: water beetles and algae asleep for months have sprung to life. The multitude of desert seeds, such as chia, sleeping dry and "dead" for years, have swollen and surrounded themselves with sticky mucilage to protect the life within them as they sprout. The boulders suddenly are slick with algae strands which undulate in the current. Water striders, insects which walk on surface tension, have suddenly found water where water was not. Bird volume has increased tenfold.

I am down there in an instant. On my hands and knees, armpit-deep, I plunge my whole skull in. Cold water goes up my nose, down my neck. Cold desert water!

Cooled down, finally, I scramble with all four limbs up through shed-sized boulders and native palms. I watch the water pulse below me through eight-foot-tall carrizo reeds. Bow Willow Canyon narrows darkly; on its steep sides, talus teeters straight up for hundreds of feet. I scramble, up and down, over and through these great stone slabs. A pearly gray California tree frog sits perfectly camouflaged on the quartz monzonite stone; I have heard their lovely Ukrainian choir at dusk.

At sixteen hundred feet, something is happening to the vegetation—the higher I climb, the more plants come into bloom. A Costa's hummingbird zaps by me at impossible velocity, stopping where it finds a solid profusion of red-orange tube flowers—a chuparosa shrub, *Justicia californica*.

At seventeen hundred feet, I discover something amazing.

Mountain chaparral—a sugar bush, deep and shiny green like manzanita—which grows at thirty-five hundred feet in the coastal mountain transition zone, appears down here at seventeen hundred feet. I am in a classic ecotone, a transition between one ecosystem and another. In the middle of the steep canyon, rock pools, cool temperatures, and tall reeds have created a microclimate.

After the dry, pricking tans of the desert arroyo, suddenly I'm walking into a Technicolor land of the living. I find a misted hanging rock garden next to a seven-foot waterfall lush with chuparosa, desert apricot, desert rock pea, water-logged mosses, and California cloak fern, *Notholaena californica*. Ferns are supposed to exist in moist forests, yet here they are in glorious desert conditions. I strip off my pack, stinky bandanna, and boots, then lie back in the waterfall's spray and dibble my toes in the lucid brown pool. Up close to my eyeballs, ferns studded with water have sprung from cracks in solid stone. To protect themselves from summer's harsh heat, they grow furry white hairs on top and exude wax underneath.

Paradise at eighteen hundred feet. The next twenty-two hundred feet promise to be a bleak boulder-scramble. Wisdom is the better part of desert travel. This is as far as I'm going.

Dawn in the In-ko-pah Badlands. In spite of their starkness, I find the "badlands" quite beautiful.

The 7,700 acres of Picacho Peak Wilderness, on the California border of Arizona near Mexico, begin as a massive wall of dark mountains. The landscape then drops into small peaks and open basins, then onto a gentle bench-land divided by hundreds of swiftly down-cut arroyos. The lowest end, near the Colorado River, holds natural rock *tinajas* (tanks) and dry waterfalls which trap rainwater from desert cloudbursts and support a healthy herd of bighorn sheep. Wild horses still roam here, and the endangered desert tortoise burrows into the volcanic earth.

The Ancient Ones walked hundreds of miles up into this wilderness from the Colorado River, then through the Carrizo Corridor, and on to the coast. Prehistoric commerce trails wound up through these badlands from the rich river bottomland, past the thin-finned ridge of dark breccia that eroded into Picacho Peak. They left their sacred images, enigmatic and evocative, hidden in the cliffs along the way.

When I begin my journey twenty miles west and high above the Colorado, the arroyo sand lies many feet deep. It's a pain to walk on: one step forward is two steps backward. My calf muscles will let me know about this tomorrow. Around the first bend, however, the high, flat desert changes, and I am in a different world, down in slot canyons which twist barely ten, sometimes forty, feet wide and fifty feet high. Up one slot and down another I memorize my way, through the maze architecture and passageways to inner sanctums. Two old palo verde trees with white-flaking trunks twisted by wind and flash flood create a thick nest for an entire food chain of animals. A whirring, buzzing, and singing emits from within this microcosm, indicating that insects, rodents, reptiles, birds, and the occasional fox or coyote have found a haven in its protective arms. All around me gape tafoni, holes formed in the loose conglomerate cliffs when a rock falls out—as enticing to me as game show prize doors. Who lives there?

The diversity of stones in this conglomerate! Rhyolite, the dry, tan matrix, is embedded with the pinks,

One comes suddenly upon desert pools of water caught in stone basins or tinajas.

Walls of Eyes and Ears

PICACHO PEAK WILDERNESS AREA

whites, reds, and patterns of granite, quartz, gneiss, and jasper. It reminds me of my grandmother's century-old button box, in which any color or pattern, shape, or texture might churn to the surface. Elsewhere in Picacho, one finds chalcedony roses, chrysocolla with malachite and cuprite, and calcite onyx.

"Alas, poor Yorick," I pronounce, holding up the carapace of a desert tortoise. As huge as a dinner platter, its worn shell indicates that it lived a long life. Its green-armored scutes are attached to the bony sleeve like snap-on, pentagonal puzzle pieces. I peer into the shell at rotting ligaments clinging to a few last leg bones and imagine its wrinkled, armored arms pulling solemnly across the sand.

"Alas, poor us," I mutter in grief. The desert tortoise, *Xeropheric agassizzii*, used to be as plentiful as a thousand per square mile over much of the desert. But after years of being riddled with bullets, run over by off-road vehicles, having their burrows collapsed by cows, drowning in mine tailings pools, and becoming infected by respiratory diseases introduced by pet tortoises, their population is declining by as much as 50 percent a year. Now one seldom sees this symbol of the desert's longevity.

But there is hope. These new wilderness areas will be tire-free, except for the enforcement or rescue vehicles of the Bureau of Land Management. I rode for a long, spine-pulverizing day with BLM enforcement officer Don Simons, and learned the challenges that face their staff: the risks of desert rescue, the extensive Emergency Medical Technician training required, and the long, frustrating hours of educating an unthinking or immature public that does not understand the murderous impact of its wheels.

Picacho Peak Wilderness begins near the Colorado River and rises to volcanic peaks.

Soon I grow impatient to be out of these narrow slot canyons. Forgetting my wilderness manners of stealth and observation, I plunge impulsively into a zone of seventy-foot-high, volcanic ash walls sculpted as intricately as Indian temple carvings. Hole after hole scooped out by erosion—each one a bit smaller than the next—are stacked on top of one another in every side canyon, creating the illusion of carved dancing figures twining in columns.

There! In a *nichos*, a recess shaped like an up-ended, Hindu eye, is a diamond-shaped face peering down at me, eyes half shut for camouflage—a kit fox sits serenely, like a small, furry Buddha.

SLOT CANYONS

The slot canyon, a quintessential form of desert architecture, is created when water cuts down through volcanic ash, sandstone, limestone, granite, or metamorphic rock. S-curved canyon walls, as sinuous as sidewinders, parallel one another, sometimes entrenched hundreds of feet deep into the earth. Inside, you can wander through labyrinths of solid rock.

Although their mouths may be as wide as soccer fields, slot canyons eventually squeeze into narrow channels. At times, a hiker must slide, back to rock, belly to rock, through walls almost as old as the bottom of the Grand Canyon or as young as a few decades. Some canyons offer ledges for foot and hand holds for escape, but others are as seamless as the water that made them. Sometimes the sky disappears. Sometimes the ground disappears.

A phenomenon of arid regions, slot canyons form when the stream channel cuts downward faster than it does laterally. Heavy downpours of rain in nearby mountain ranges funnel into existing fault lines in the surface of the earth where they flow down into the cracks rather than spread out over the surface as they might do in the Midwest. Large volumes of swiftly moving sediment rapidly carve out mudstone, siltstone, and conglomerate and slowly chisel down through metamorphosed schists and gneiss. The carving tool is not merely water but a liquid concrete containing everything from fine sediment to huge boulders, depending upon the velocity and carrying capacity of the flood.

Flash floods are most frequent in summer, when the hard-baked ground is least absorbent and water carves with unbridled power. Water slams against obstacles with a force of sixty-four times its own weight; flash floods compound this cutting power by traveling twenty to forty miles per hour. Ironically, a leading cause of death in the desert is drowning. Suddenly materializing "out of nowhere," flash floods are capable of sweeping heavy vehicles off the road complete with children, ice coolers, and the family dog.

When hiking in slot canyons, always watch the weather in the adjacent mountains: even though it is cloudless overhead, a slot canyon can quickly turn into one great Waring blender if it rains in the high country. A sound like thunder or a distant freight train can signal a coming flash flood. If you are caught, climb as high and as quickly as you can up onto side terraces on the inside of a curve; here the current has less velocity. Never attempt to cross a flash flood.

I remember once standing with my mouth wide open in a wide valley in Denali National Park, Alaska, as a nine-foot-tall wall of gray churning liquid roared down the dry stream bed, bashing into old debris and moving boulders as I scrambled aside. Although this flash flood was caused by an ice dam breaking somewhere high in a glacier, the terror down in my gut was the same as it would have been had I been caught in the path of a desert flash flood.

The agave's juicy roots, its thick, blue-green leaves, and tall, laden flower stalk prompted one Native American observer to remark, "Look at all that food!"

I hold my breath and freeze my motion, not wishing to disturb him. The fifteen inch tall, red-and-white fox remains frozen. I ever so slowly sit down and remain cross-legged before it, observing closely for twenty minutes. The fox-Buddha does not move an eyelash. I sit for another twenty minutes, watching for his breath, examining every muscle and curve; still the kit fox does not move. Finally, with no effort at all, he flows like silk out the hole and straight up the cliff.

Humbled now, because I had been too fast and clumsy in my movements before, I become keenly aware of the labyrinths of life these canyons hold in every nook and cranny. I stalk quietly, one breath, two steps. At each overhang, I kneel and examine the insect, bird, and four-legged tracks which unlock the secrets of animal interaction like a Rosetta stone. Enthralled, it dawns on me that every one of these holes, each arch of old tree, each hollowed out cholla holds a unique culture of beings.

It is darker. Pocketed free-tailed bats, *Tadarida femorosacca*, dive by my head with a high squeal. I am delighted—bats are essential to the life of the desert; some pollinate plants and others eat huge quantities of insects. I breathe upward to let them know who I am.

I become aware of the arroyos being covered with eyes and ears and other sense organs I can't even imagine—those that feel vibrations or pick up my body molecules. The forked tongues of snakes, the noses of foxes, the ground sensors in bird legs, the ears . . . hundreds of thousands of ears, all listening. I feel like a monster in size-nine boots clomping through fragile spheres.

Completely entranced by this complex labyrinth of animals, I have lost my sense of the outside world. My concentration is suddenly ripped apart by the roar of military helicopters not fifty feet above me. After they are gone, I think of the shattering noise of two-stroke engines, the gross crunch of spinning tires, the fingernail squeak of mesquite branch on metal. All this comes ripping into the fragile, four-dimensional web of sound and smell on which desert fauna depend for dinner, safety, moisture, and mating.

I imagine myself as a moth or a bat. Each mechanical roar mutilates my delicate web of night scent, vibration, and subtle magnetic fields. It shreds my nighttime radar, it gasses the pheromones of my whirring insect lover. Next year, I know there will be fewer of us to pollinate the flowers. Then fewer flowers. The desert will grow bare.

Suddenly I look up. It has become too dark to see. Dusk wraps the canyons in lavender scrims. I imagine secret chambers of the arroyos springing open as I leave: kangaroo rats, owls, coyotes, bats, herds of male tarantulas in search of love.

The Picacho Peak formation was laid down as volcanic breccia layers, then it eroded away into stark peaks and spires.

With two gallons of water in my backpack, in the heat of midday, I grunt up this trail through badlands, across thin ridges where the crumbling sediment drops off to either side. From the Picacho Peak Wilderness, I have driven due west seventy miles to the Coyote Mountain Wilderness, adjacent to Anza-Borrego State Park. A narrow dirt trail shoots steeply up through mineral-rich, ocher-yellow, conical foothills. This is the passage to the Coyotes' secret upper basins.

Not too long ago in geological time, the Coyote Mountains rose in a massive lump, then eroded down to the east and west from the middle. To the east is a spectacular "painted" gorge, and to the west is the steep grade of Fossil Canyon, criss-crossed by an intricate, dendritic maze of deep arroyos. At each bend, hundreds of grottos have been gutted out at the outswing of flash floods through soft sediment. Each bend holds small gifts: the grotto, a fossil, the footprints of the night. I search for the flesh-hued barefoot gecko, a rare and beautiful night lizard, but he is not to be seen. Not yet, not here.

Seeing the myriad natural grottos, I realize how alive this desert is. It is one long apartment-house dwelling after another, one on top of another. After an hour of trudging, I spy the wind caves high in the tops of the Coyotes. Some are cut clear through twenty feet of solid white granite. Time and a fine wind have created these organic, feminine spaces. Seen from below, the wind tunnels are smooth ovoids, mouthlike and animated with an intelligent force, while down in the slot canyon, the grottos are ragged-edged.

I come to a dry waterfall and must climb around it with my sixty-pound pack. I climb another four hundred feet to a hard white sandstone shelf with dark brown knobs, little pedestals embedded with huge conch shells which look as if they were preserved yesterday. Cell by cell, each shell was slowly replaced with stone in solution.

The crumbling matrix of granitic rock is carried away by the ever-present wind, creating sensuous shapes.

A Moonful Night in the Wind Caves

THE COYOTE MOUNTAINS

Beautiful spirals, cones, and "roses" of shell fossils six million years old lie in jagged-edged form. Although I find an exquisite scallop shell, I resist taking it home. These fossils hold their magic in place, not disintegrating in some forgotten basket in a faraway state. Too many thoughtless people have picked this place clean; it is essential to leave treasures for others to find.

After climbing for three hours, I find myself finally up near the wind caves. Their origin seems impossible until I crawl inside and feel the wind howling through. Nearby, layers of smooth, fine-grained stone alternate with a cataclysmic tumble of coarse-grained, dark sandstone embedded with whole clusters of shells and animal tube castings, as if trapped by a massive landslump into the ancient sea.

The wind holes, with their ragged lips and jagged teeth made of this harder sandstone, look like old crones trying to keep secrets from the young winds who hollow out their interiors.

Eerie. Eerie. In late November the light fails early, and I feel anxious. Throwing my bag on a wind-swept saddle between the wind caves and huge, bulbous stone turrets, I gaze and gaze at the Carrizo Badlands below me, which darkness will soon sponge into flat monotones. Badlands, contrary to their name, are excruciatingly beautiful. Most are striped in horizontal layers: deep gold on the bottom, light gold on top, or bright red with white tops. What was once earth's core minerals, thrust up into mountains, is now encoded and translated into smooth, lyrical layers.

Humans are deeply drawn to badlands, to the archetype of labyrinth within them—mazes so complex they would confound the Greek Minotaur. These badlands tumble down in conical heaps which hide deep slot canyons. During flash floods, tremendous sediment loads are carried out toward Carrizo Wash and then to the Salton Sea. From here, one can see the entire terrain, clear up to the Santa Rosa Mountains, over to the Chocolate Mountains near the Arizona border and the Salton Sea's basin, an extension of the Gulf of Mexico trough.

* * *

I love to solve earth puzzles. In the desert they are clearer than anywhere else on the planet—the bare-bones of a Rubik's Cube in four or five dimensions. Here's the recipe: take immense layers of time and twist. Fold them over, point them straight upward. Slice into a grid of fault lines and

From my bedroll on a high Coyote Mountain saddle, I gazed north into the Carrizo Badlands, the Fish Creek Mountains, and far beyond to the Salton Sea.

shake rapidly. Squeeze. Bake the surface at up to 138 degrees repeatedly

What grandeur comes of faulting and warping! The badlands rise and fall in a sea of the maximum chop, like intersecting waves. Just six million years ago, they were a flat plane of sea sediment, colorful layer upon layer hidden beneath a benign dullness. Later, when the land began to lift as the earth's plates shifted, they eroded in maximum relief; now no slope is less than 50 degrees perpendicular. My bedroom-cliff is a fault's vertical escarpment—an abrupt face which plunges a thousand feet down to the Carrizo Badlands.

To the east, Painted Gorge cuts down deeply into an unseen chasm, exposing a tumble of blacks and grays and whites and lavenders, with near-vertical slopes in rust-white-rust layers. I wish I could rappel down into its spasms of hues. At 5:07, dusk, it is all dark below the thousand-foot drop-off, yet the sun is casting the upturned sediments above a brilliant orange. In this peculiar lighting, I notice a wind cave eighty feet above me. One half of the cave is precisely sealed with careful stone work. At its entrance, the rock drops straight down, making it a dangerous and dubious place to sleep. Groping my way around to the other side of the huge sandstone outcrop in the dark, I discover that the access is still a scary technical climb with dangerous exposure, about eighty feet straight down.

Back in my bag, I obsess on the origin of the cave's stone work. Who built that wall and how long ago? The huge stone arch over it appears as a crouched figure which becomes more and more animated in the fading light. This has telltale signs of being a shaman's cave, of which there are many in these desert mountains. I fall asleep with the katabatic breezes of the desert mountains blowing through the electric zig-zags of the ten-foot-tall spikes of ocotillo overhead.

An hour later, I come suddenly awake. The wind has ceased, and the night smells intensify in the cold air: dusty, moist, organic, and vividly alive. As I lie there, feet pointing northeast, a huge orange disk of moon rises up through them as if my toes were on fire. I lie perfectly still and listen acutely. A profound "spiritual entertainment" comes from the natural sounds and smells which wrap around my body in this desert night. Falling half asleep, I relive my journey upward: a huge jackrabbit walked slowly out of my way. I followed coyote tracks. The loggerhead shrike on an ocotillo impaled a wriggling insect on a sharp spike. All is well-nigh perfect.

The fractious moon casts light all over, making it as bright as an overcast day back home in Washington State. Such a winter moon lends a feeling of dormancy, a lack of life's frenzied, symbiotic loops of buzzing insect, flower, bird, and beast. Now all underground, stored in roots, huddled in hope, or paused in hibernation, the flora and fauna of the desert await their February spring. But not quite all.

I awake again in a frenzied state; a creature like a raccoon stops to gawk at my face, but adjusting to moonlight, I find he is not a raccoon at all. He is catlike, with the curiosity of a predator, and has strange white rings around its eyes. A ringtail! Up close, his woolly tail is partially circled in black. He sleeps by day and hunts small animals by night. Had I not slept here, I would never have seen him,

STILL WILD, ALWAYS WILD

The Santa Rosa is a very young mountain range—Its ridgeline has not yet eroded into sharp peaks and canyons.

and I am still not sure that he was not an apparition.

       I gaze out again at the badlands, which seem to be filled with creatures of the night. I think I can see eye shine in various places, gleaming yellow or white. Or is this merely unexploded ordnance from the Carrizo Impact Area bombing range seven miles north? The eye shine moves from place to place.

       Finally, a snub-nosed sun streaks the badlands and the Fish Creek Mountains to the north a rosy, viscous orange. Within the steep badlands mounds, stark, comb-toothed shadows call to me to come explore deep within them. The sun now lights up the rock wall with all the wind caves. The shaman's cave is alight with direct sunlight, yet seems no less inexplicable. Now I can see that the area in front of it is worn down from repeated use, and yet no animal would be so crazy as to den up there with such exposure.

       I pack up my bag in under twelve minutes and hit the trail, anxious to explore the deepest, most lovely slot canyon. At 9:30, I am dropping down rapidly through gneiss and other swirling metaphoric rocks. I drop five hundred feet in under a quarter of a mile, down-climbing boulders the size of VW bugs. The walls soon loom three hundred feet above me, red rock rippling like cellulite bumps. Deeper and deeper I drop, until the walls come together and meander only an arm's length apart. Finally I am under a wedge of rock the size of an office building which fell from high in the Coyotes thousands of years ago. As I wedge underneath it through a narrow crotch of stone, I am warily convinced that this is the moment it will finish its fall.

       Quite suddenly, I am spewed out into the mouth of this slot canyon. The boulders tossed by flash floods disappear. In their place is a soft sand bottom filled with desert holly, desert milkweed, and blooming desert trumpet. The unscalable sides of the badlands canyons slope upward steeply in the golden tans I had seen from high above. So this is what it feels like to be inside the Carrizo Badlands, I think, and curl up in their cool, damp shade.

       I wish I could wander forever through these immense conical hills, perfect as breasts, richly hued as Navajo weavings. If I wander too far out, I will be within the Carrizo Bombing Range amid unexploded ordnance. The dry sediments are sucking moisture from my skin. It is time to return.

HOW WIND CAVES ARE FORMED

Aligned with the path of a constant and prevailing wind, wind caves begin as slight indentations where the wind catches again and again. There, new rock surface is constantly exposed as the wind removes exfoliated flakes of granite or grains of sandstone which have been weakened by percolating water.

       Wind cave formation and placement are determined by four factors: the rock type, the surface permeability, the mineral structure within the rock, and the wind's direction and force.

       Throughout the desert are sills and dikes, handsome veins of igneous crystals that run through finer-grained, quickly cooled rock. The fractures between their crystalline surfaces break down faster than the surrounding rock, creating tubular holes for the work of the wind.

       The white granite of the Coyotes' caves crumbles its matrix of plastioclastic feldspar into clay, leaving loose flakes of mica, iron, and quartz. I scoop these up in my palm and let the glittering minerals drift through my fingers.

       On many elevated ridges of many desert mountain ranges, I can find wind caves in which I can curl up and listen to the wind howling through from an ancient time, on its way to an ancient place.

The sand arroyo ahead of me vibrates with heat waves. I'm only seven miles in on a twenty-five-mile, three-day journey to Rockhouse Canyon, and it is already too hot. I concentrate, putting one foot in front of the other. The white sand could be as deep as two hundred feet. It is soft. I am walking in slow motion while expending a runner's energy, carrying three gallons of liquid in my thirty-year-old Kelty pack.

Luminous datura trumpets, Georgia O'Keeffe's gramophone-shaped blossoms—fourteen inches long and vivid white—sing to me like Enrico Caruso from the damp shadows. I am driven by legend—someone has mentioned, just briefly, the site of a Cahuilla village whose occupancy stretched from prehistory to the 1930s. The stone foundations, I am told, can still be seen.

Rockhouse Canyon begins as a quarter-mile-wide arroyo meandering from cliff to cliff. Each meander-wavelength takes its time, like toothless old men wandering a town with nowhere to go. Each meander requires twenty minutes of slogging, only to turn and give view to the same long meander going the opposite way. And another. And another. I plod for four miles of soft sand before reaching the canyon; the sun drills holes in my skull.

I slump down on a damp sand bank next to a huge datura. Outrageous spider wasps, tarantula hawks, *Hemipepsis*—black-bodied but with brilliant orange, two-inch wings—swarm by the hundreds over a tall shrub with pale green flowers. Scrambling through a guidebook, I learn that adults drink nectar, but raise their young in a carrion nursery. The female spreads a spider between her legs, swiftly digs a burial chamber, and deposits the spider and her eggs inside. The larvae have infinite sack lunches until they are old enough to escape their cradle-grave.

The oxidation of minerals in stone paints the desert with vivid color.

Singing a Mountain Home

INTO ROCKHOUSE CANYON

Symbiosis is the most elegant concept in nature; all life evolved symbiotically, including human beings. Such an elegant relationship lies between the tarantula hawk and its food, a ten-foot-tall shrub with gray-green stems and flowers. Since these pale, army green blossoms smell wretched, I wonder to what other sense the bush appeals to attract hungry tarantula hawks who pollinate it in return. How many eons has it taken to form this peculiar interdependence? Who made the first move, wasp or flower? Who took that first long kiss that was to perpetuate both of them down through the epochs?

The sky now fills so thickly with brilliant butterflies that it turns more orange than blue. It has been a hellaciously fecund year for *Vanessa cardii*, painted ladies butterflies; millions coat the tall, fragrant lavender bushes nearby. Again and again I attempt to photograph an orange bush, but painted ladies are primordially triggered to fly a split second before a shutter click. Again and again the bush turns lavender in my viewfinder.

Soon, my bare, motionless legs are confronted by a thirteen-inch, shrunken stegosaur with a pugnacious sense of humor. As a child I followed reptiles intrepidly on hands and knees but never caught a one. A zebra tail lizard, with its striking black-and-white tail pattern, ripples by my feet. A delicate fringe-toed lizard swims downward into the sand when he smells my presence with his stereo-olfactory tongue, which flips odiferous molecules from sand to vomeronasal organs in the roof of his mouth. These small, bulbed cavities once connected to an external nose, but now it has disappeared.

It is hard to explain why I would strap on sixty pounds and walk through 90-degree heat merely to visit a canyon where nobody lives anymore. It is, for me, a form of storytelling: my legs are the narrator, and my heart is the listener. Across the Sonoran Desert, seasonal and long-term Native American villages are marked by stone circles, house foundations, *manos* and *metates* for grinding grain, and sacred rock art, often near springs. While standing in a wind-swept Sonoran landscape, it is difficult to imagine an isolated site as a thriving Cahuilla Indian urban center. Yet here, four desert ecosystems, from low desert to subalpine mountain, offered the people food, shelter, and great beauty.

The Santa Rosa addition protects the springs and rich riparian zones of Coyote and Rockhouse Canyons.

The position of a desert village was determined by the presence of water, proximity to food-gathering areas, and lines of commerce. Natural formations became sacred sites. Often, if resources were limited, favorable locations were occupied by just one clan. In areas of abundance, however, several family groups would live together, sharing the land and using it according to instructions from their hereditary songs and visions.

Cahuilla villages were active places of commerce, work, storytelling, shamanistic healing and rites, and on the vine-wing-and-hoof grocery shopping. The magnificent topography did not escape the villager's eye: all rock art, village sites, and Cahuilla life was created within and in response to its surroundings.

Rockhouse Canyon rises over its fourteen miles through four environmental zones, up a narrowing canyon into a high Santa Rosa Mountain basin. Cahuilla village sites often included Lower Sonoran, Upper Sonoran, the Transition Zone—and they moved into coniferous forests—and, at nine thousand feet, the Mountain Zone. Today these sites would still provide a great variety and volume of food to eat.

After five miles, I am delighted to watch the rock walls of the canyon vising inward, the rite of passage from one ecosystem to the next. The sudden altitude gain is like a miniature birth, squeezing me unscathed from one world into the next while gulping air. I am short of breath and dripping sweat.

Rockhouse Canyon is the secret passage into a Southern California of a century ago, into a Cahuilla village nestled in gentle mountains with no road. Even by horse the trek is difficult: no water for fourteen miles. Its sheer rock walls have kept Jeeps and their terrible offspring, all-terrain vehicles, from entrance. To earn it, you walk.

I am an avid searcher of edges. Watching for ecosystem shifts is like watching someone age; it can happen in dramatic spurts or in movements too slow to perceive. As Rockhouse Canyon rises rapidly, the walls turn from unconsolidated river delta sediments to solid stone, forming a geological edge. Plant life changes quickly in response to new soil and altitude. Merging ecosystems, called ecotones, offer rich biodiversity.

As I climb, I see willows which signal underground water. Brown-eyed primrose, prickly poppy, and datura blooms indicate an underground river. *Cholla hoggmannii*, a scraggly cholla indigenous only to one locale—Anza-Borrego of Southern California—blooms luminous yellow. Bladderpods, mallow, tamarisks, and hundreds of barrel cactus species mark the beginning of the Upper Sonoran Ecosystem.

Higher and higher I climb up the canyon stairway. Sweat pours down past my bandanna, picking up salt, dirt, army-surplus bug juice, and sunscreen along the way, then oozes into my eyes. I have a surreal, dizzy sensation as I look at ocotillos growing tall and skinny up the canyon walls. They zap up from the earth as a boy draws wavy lines outward to symbolize a bomb exploding; their brilliant orange-flowered points seem capable of making percussive noises.

STILL WILD, ALWAYS WILD

The smoke tree is a gray-green-stemmed tree that carries on photosynthesis in its bark. It is used by native people for fuel, shade, and ornament.

Ocotillo, *Fouquieria splendens*, are surreal. Skinny twelve-foot stalks originate from one point in the sand, branchless and full of sharp thorns. These are not cactus, and the thorns are not thorns but petioles, the leaf stems left as each leaf drops off to conserve moisture in the dry season. Instantly these leaves reappear at the first rain, taking advantage of any moisture, so the plants may have many "spring" blooms in a wet year. Ocotillo belong to an unusual family of only eleven or so species, mostly Mexican, that includes the rare boojum tree, *Idria columnaris*, found only in Baja California, Mexico. At their tips, a brass section of tubular, flame-colored flowers blare visually like Mariachi trumpets.

Above me, tall plumes of agaves, screwbeans, catclaws, pencil cactus, ironwood trees, and mistletoe scribble their branches against the eroding desert hills. In my eyes, the Most-Elegant-Design winner is screwbean mesquite, *Prosopis pubescens*, adorned with spiraled pods like polished caterpillars. I try tapping these coiled springs, expecting that they will go zinging off into space, rockets of coiled energy. They don't. They will drop prosaically, by themselves, in summer and unwind with slow decorum, releasing hundreds of small bean seeds.

Seeds are a plant's songs from ancestor to ancestor, from grandmother to mother to grandchild. The Old Ones, the Cahuilla women, knew that songs deep within each species told each new plant exactly what to do or to be: when to bloom, what color to be, when to go to seed. Even when a seed travels far away in a flood, or lives in a dark place for a hundred years . . . even then, when it sprouts, it remembers its songs.

Night Covers the Sky with a Cracked Bowl

Where one-hundred-foot rock walls choke inward, a clump of twenty-year-old hikers gather around what has to be Hidden Springs. I never depend on springs marked on a desert map, especially ones called "hidden." They too often turn out to be moaning, sunburned, three-inch patches of brown water thick with bees—like this one. The young hikers warn me sternly to carry water into the canyon, as if the thought had never occurred to me. They look ready to drop from thirst and nausea.

As the day ages, heat and hikers disappear. The best part of my journey begins: solitude. Metamorphic rock pinches inward; somewhere the canyon walls have slipped from unconsolidated sea sediment into ominously dark gneiss. Gneiss, a metamorphic stone of quartz, feldspar, and mica or hornblend, evokes solemnity in me as I plod through its damp shadow. It is intricately patterned, like illuminated manuscripts.

Dusk pours into Rockhouse Canyon like a liquid. It smells of moldy ledgers. Although slightly frightened, I am also thrilled. Bats frenetically dart, and a cottontail freezes inches from me. Out of the corner of my eye, a kit fox draws the edge of my perception into my awareness. The downward spiral of the canyon wren's ethereal song gives me goose bumps—it is the quintessential sound of the desert.

The walls now rise four hundred feet, cinching inward. I boulder hop across patterned stones three feet in diameter. When this canyon-trough does fill with water, the flood's velocity will

In late March and early April, the desert explodes with saturated color, such as this blooming hedgehog cactus.

chew up everything in its path. I scan the unscalable walls for escape routes. I start thinking about making a bed, but I don't want to sleep here: a flash flood could easily pour down from the high Santa Rosas.

By now, it is dark down in the bottom. I come to a dry, hundred-foot water chute. Climbing its vertical face of polished granite is impossible. I heard that a Jeep club had once winched Jeeps up the side of it, having built a stairway out of huge slabs. Why? Why pound your thirty-thousand-dollar investment to smithereens, pound on Mother Nature, and risk breaking down in the middle of nowhere? Fortunately, Mother Nature shook the earth soon afterward and made the chute completely impassable again. Cautiously, I arrange boot edge after boot edge up the slickrock.

On top of the precipitous rock shoulder above the water chute, there is just enough sand for one short person to lie down, but no more. Having clambered out of the underworld, I crawl into my sleeping bag and write. Too tired to eat, I take out pen, nibs, and ink and literally draw closure on my day.

The changing of the guard takes place at this crepuscular hour: bats come flushing out of rock holes to search for specific flowers—again, symbiosis. The night is intense with fragrance in the denser air; scent molecules reach my nose more readily now than during the heat of the day. I wander the craters of the full moon through my binoculars.

This day has been deeply satisfying: I have identified thirty-seven new (to me) plants and been stumped by fifteen more. The endless forms that flora take enchant me; looking at them is like seeing nature's deepest imagination unfold.

In the morning, I plan to make it far back into a deserted Cahuilla village, then to live there for several days, undisturbed by living human beings, listening to whatever the Cahuilla ancestors have to teach me.

For a long while, I gaze down the valley fifty miles away through O'Keeffian, eroded, arroyo edge mounds of zippered red and white stripes. Such intertoothing, like two hair combs whose teeth have been pushed together, is a common pattern left by the flash floods. The heavily laden water slams down the canyon from side to side in a zig-zag, leaving sharp mounds on either side.

Life is simple, clean. Throw a cloth on the ground, drink water, sit silently, no thoughts.

The desert agave offers an abundance for native people: sweet buds for roasting; leaf fibers for rope, cloth, and shoes; and an intoxicating liquor. It is a condo and supermarket for insect and bird life.

Driving due north from the Santa Rosa Mountains, I reach the 24,200-acre Mecca Hills Wilderness Area, which contains an unusual geological labyrinth. The Mecca Hills are a world-class anticline, a twenty-mile-wide V of Cenozoic era (up to sixty-five-million-year-old) stone eroded from an older, larger version of the Little San Bernardino Mountains. The anticline was squeezed upward with pressure from the San Andreas fault and Blue Cut fault. This arch of soft, badland strata, which runs along the base of the Little San Bernardinos, was rapidly cut down into a maze. Colorful layers of mud breccia, volcanic ash, and sandstone are ideally pliant, both for folding and for rapid slot canyon formation. These strata give geologists important clues about the impact of earthquakes and faulting in Southern California—in their down-sliced mazes of exposed sediment, geologists can read the history of structural movement like an open book.

Now, through the scrim of smoke tree, ironwood, and mesquite, I watch the Salton Sea turn into a silver pillow which swells above the horizon in the distance. It is so beautiful in this sub-sea-level illusion that it seems impossible to me it could be a dying sea, filled with agricultural chemicals and salts from the surrounding mountains. A dead sea has almost no life, and it stinks when one is within a mile of it.

The Mecca Hills' colors are breathtaking and complex. To the north, a gray carpet of loose sediments sprawls into deep folds six hundred feet high. To the west, a mesa pours brick red sediment down the dozens of vertical arroyos cut in an underlying layer of soft white: it appears as long fringes of rain in a pale desert sky. Behind the mesa, soft moss-yellow hills underline farther gray mesas cut through with swirls of eggplant-hued embroidery.

Soon I enter the narrow canyons where the Mecca Hills have been sliced like so much marbled beef. I climb up the maze, past silver desert holly, catclaw acacia which snags my skin, desert willow, heart-leafed primrose,

A cheese bush stands out against steep eroding Mecca Hills sediments.

Labyrinths, Bullhorns, and Double Dead Ends

THE MECCA HILLS WILDERNESS AREA

Oenothera cardiophylla, and the foul-smelling cheese bush. Past palo verde's yellow blooms, past soft mounds of desert velvet, and the scraggly haired fagonia with its blooms like a spray of scattered purple stars.

Suddenly I look up and see giant blocks of sandstone the weight of cement-loaded Ford pickups balancing precariously above me. If the Blue Cut fault slips, I'll be dead meat.

I climb up through the slot canyon which narrows again and again until it seems impossible that it could narrow anymore. I can touch both sides at once. Climbing up through piles of shed-sized rubble, I am being tossed over the double horns of claustrophobia and exhilaration. At last, the double dead end of this labyrinth: two thirty-foot-tall, cylindrical water chutes of breccia and sandstone. I glimpse up at two semicircles of sky.

Up on a last shelf, I find myself in a dilemmic dead end. If I had jackrabbit–sized leg muscles, I could spring into the gracious light of late afternoon. Tomorrow I will continue up the enormous six-thousand-foot Blue Cut escarpment more prosaically—in a truck—crossing the ecotone between the Sonoran and Mojave Deserts.

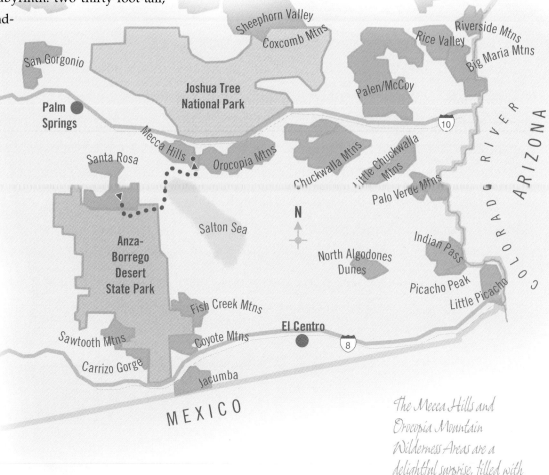

The Mecca Hills and Orocopia Mountain Wilderness Areas are a delightful surprise, filled with deeply eroded slot canyons and intense hues of rock strata.

At the entrance to the Mecca Hills anticline, the brick red, oxidized sediments pour down into the soft white layer below.

ANTICLINES AND SYNCLINES

The earth's crust is in constant motion. It shrinks, stretches apart, and moves laterally or vertically as in mountain building, called orogeny, takes place. When the earth's surface area must shrink, because of the compression of two tectonic plates, its pliant crust deforms by tilting, folding, and warping. Warps form best in soft sedimentary layers which can move across one another with little friction. An anticline is an arch upward with the most ancient rocks in the center.

Sealed at the ends like a kayak, they often trap water, oil, and gas. A large anticline can be hundreds of miles long and thousands of feet deep.

Synclines, on the other hand, are concave folds like a trough. Outer layers of sediment slope away from their center. Bend a sheaf of mulit-colored paper. Imagine slicing each side off at an angle, thus revealing the various colors, or strata, and you have the geologic effect. Each of the strata took hundreds of thousands of years to be deposited, either from volcanic debris or sediments worn off of neighboring mountains.

Stormlight in the Orocopia Mountains.

I am driving and rising rapidly through Box Canyon, thirty miles into that great twisted jumble of Joshua Tree National Park geology. Its huge slabs of white tank quartz monzonite and pinto gneiss—crosscut by andesite and rhyolite dikes—have been burned into the American consciousness. The Joshua Tree landscape is so much a part of our heritage that creating it as a national park is long overdue. Joshua Tree has been expanded from 559,000 acres to 793,000 acres, 630,000 of which are designated as wilderness. To the northeast hover the Coxcomb Mountains, shaped like their thin namesake; to the southeast, Eagle Mountain's riparian habitat; and to the southwest, the steep drainages of the Little San Bernardino Mountains—all complete ecosystems. Noncontiguous, but essential and extraordinarily beautiful, are the Mecca Hills and Orocopia Wilderness Areas just south of Interstate 10, consisting of endless slot canyons to explore.

Joshua Tree's stadium-sized mounds of granitic quartz monzonite have eroded over thousands of years along a three-dimensional grid of faulting and cracking. Although these blocks give the suggestion of being tossed like dominoes, they have actually been weathered out of a solid mass of molten intrusions, called plutons, which underlie the park. Joshua Tree is a rock climber's paradise, crawling with dazzling, Lycra-clad, youthful bodies that jingle with carabiners and slings. There are too damned many humans here for my taste.

After spending the day clambering around the huge granite boulders, I drive up to Keys Overlook to gaze down a breath-stopping drop of six thousand feet toward the Mecca Hills, the Orocopia Mountains, and the Salton Sea. From below sea level up to 5,814-foot Quail Mountain in the north, this escarpment along the east-west Blue Cut fault marks the transition between the Colorado Sonoran Desert and the Mojave Desert. One can almost draw the line between ocotillo and silver cholla on the south and Joshua trees and piñon on the north.

A dike or sill of larger crystals forms when molten rock cools more slowly than the surrounding rock.

Twisted Jumble of Geology

JOSHUA TREE NATIONAL PARK

The aromatic desert smells change abruptly along with the plants.

Far to the south I can see almost to the Jacumba and Coyote Mountains behind the blinding white gleam of the Salton Sea, 274 feet below sea level. I can gaze down at the Mecca Hills' vertical sedimentary layers cut by the deep slot canyons which swallowed me yesterday. After two days of climbing around Joshua Tree and hiking up the Eagle Mountain riparian area, I am too sore to move and must be content with watching the strange light effects on the mountains to the southwest.

The cool disk of sun through snow clouds is cutting a semicircular notch down into the Santa Rosa Mountains, which rise straight up out of the desert floor to 6,666 feet. Instantly, they are transformed into a translucent sheet of gray gold Mylar: a filmy silhouette filling the western sky. These are very young mountains, as indicated by the even edge of sediments along their not-yet-eroded peaks. An electric gold outlines their silhouette. Sleeping on the overlook would be bliss, but also illegal—instead I must find a legal camping spot in an overly full national park.

Tomorrow, I think to myself with great anticipation and some trepidation, I will drive northeast 150 miles to the Old Woman Mountains.

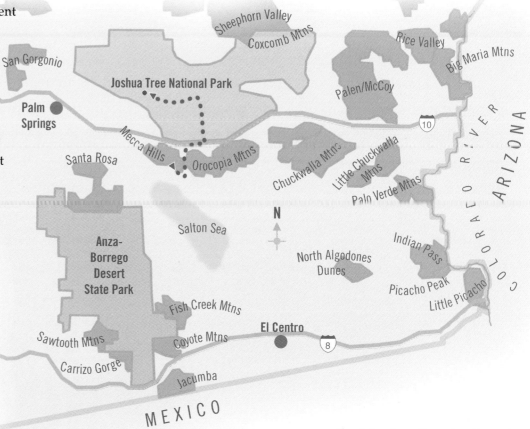

The Joshua tree is the most visible member of the local ecosystem, an entire complex of birds, lizards, and insects depend upon this plant. In turn, this yucca depends on a nocturnal moth, Pronuba sp., for pollination and, thus, its existence.

STILL WILD, ALWAYS WILD

Sunrise on brittlebush and desert pavement in the Eagle Mountains, a critical riparian habitat newly added to Joshua Tree National Park.

O f all the names of the sixty-nine newly protected desert wilderness areas, the "Old Woman Mountains" most enchanted me. I had a vague notion that the Old Woman of this 146,020-acre wilderness, thirty-five miles southwest of Needles, California, held wisdom for me from another age. My first attempts to enter these isolated, jagged mountains ended in failure because the road was too rough or time ran out, but yesterday I finally managed to get tucked twenty miles back in a most beautiful campsite. Tomorrow I leave before dawn to climb the wall of mountains which holds the Old Woman two thousand feet aloft.

A crimson rind of sun pokes over the edge of the earth, infusing twenty mountain layers to the north with twenty shades of orange, and my skin picks up the first glow of warmth. The Old Woman reigns stately above me, already drenched in millions of years of her own history. Made of granite slabs shooting two hundred feet above the ridge, this natural formation looks like a woman sitting on a stone chair with her hands in her lap, facing southeast.

Far beneath her, I begin climbing up the near-vertical mountain wall which encircles a lush valley a thousand feet below. Now, at nine o'clock, in the morning chill, the sun shoots dusty shafts of light onto the granite monoliths. Each skyscraper-sized stone shifts from dark cobalt to dusky gray to pale lavendar to rosy eggshell, then to brilliant white. This landscape intimidates me. I am frightened—not of the failure of foot or hand—but by the sheer power of these mountains and sense of the sacredness of place.

Climbing up through granite means scrambling through cracks the size of those in back of refrigerators, through holes the size of coffins under tons of fallen rock. Deep within these recesses, moss sponges and ferns touch my skin, in contrast to the dry, rough-toothed exfoliating granite. I am struck with the beauty of Parry's nolinas,

The forms and patterns created in the Old Woman Mountain granite fill my imagination with endless images.

Yoni and Pregnant Chia Seeds

THE OLD WOMAN MOUNTAINS

with their pin-striped, sword-shaped leaves and dry, seven-foot flower stalks, and Wright's buckwheat, with its delicate pink and white blooms. Catclaw acacia and desert apricot tear my clothes. Juniper grows out of vertical cracks in sheer rock.

A mourning dove gurgles; the jubilee of a black-throated sparrow overlaps with the deep *kar-rrrronk* of two ravens overhead.

The Old Woman is not the only shape of feminine divinity in these mountains. As I climb, I pass myriad wind and solution caves in pure, white granite, caves as round as pregnant women's bellies, some big enough for a whole tribe curled together, others large enough for a family, still others intimate enough for a kit fox, a mountain lion, or for one human curled in the fetal position, dreaming.

Mountain lion! Far up here on stone, my flesh goes cold to the bone— predator scat. I spy cattle thigh bones high up in the crags above the springs. Mountain lion! What am I doing up here alone?

Suddenly, I am retreating. It takes me two hours to climb down and around a jutting mountain ridge. Between two elongated layers of hard granite sixty feet long, shaped like legs draped in cloth, I discover a series of alga green, paisley-shaped pools descending in successive steps. The lower, larger, curvilinear holes hold standing water, most unusual in the desert. These are called yoni, female fertility symbols which form naturally within this stone, and they have been held as a great source of spiritual and reproductive power by ancient and contemporary people. I have heard that these mountains are still sacred to the Chemehuevi Nation, many of whose people live over near Needles now.

Such pools are formed over centuries by infinite water trickles which carry off feldspar flakes from the soft stone in between harder rock layers. This rhythm of hard-soft-hard rock layering begins deep within the earth when the granite is still a molten plug and translates on the earth's surface into a series of jade-hued, fetal-shaped pools. These pools, also known as *tinajas*, were worshiped for their water-collecting powers because water is the source of all life. Pools also supply a grand metaphor for that other source of life: women giving birth.

Access to the Old Woman Mountains proved to be a long and hard trek. The Old Woman statue sits stoically through the centuries.

Yucca and barrel cactus, Old Woman Mountains.

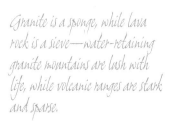

Granite is a sponge, while lava rock is a sieve—water-retaining granite mountains are lush with life, while volcanic ranges are stark and sparse.

Gazing around at this protected, two-mile-wide, upland valley, I observe that it would have made an excellent village site, and my overactive imagination peoples it with the Ancient Ones. From here, they could climb into the high mountains in summer to collect piñon nuts, and, in winter, descend to the low desert to collect chia and mesquite seeds. Here they could have beavertail prickly pear, the roots of Bigelow's or Parry's nolina, Joshua tree and yucca fruit, and abundant rodent, antelope, and bighorn sheep meat. This is a place of life-giving abundance.

I want to imagine living in such a place, so I lie down on the warm, white stone beside the pools. The radiant energy from stone passes into my limbs, and I fall into a doze-trance. I imagine myself to be a young Chemehuevi woman living five hundred years ago. I picture myself pregnant at fourteen with my first child and feel how jubilant I would be. I am also fearful, but I know many elder women who will help me through this first birth. So, too, I believe, will the Old Woman statue.

I take a real chia seed in my mouth, and as I lie there, the seed itself becomes pregnant. It swells up and coats itself with a mucilage which protects it while it is sprouting, even after many years of dormancy. I swallow it: it will be digested very slowly and will help to prevent disease. I should be grinding seeds or weaving, I tell myself in my dream state, but I am still just a child lying here making shapes out of clouds.

Far below me, I imagine I can hear the chirruping of the village children. A thousand weird rock forms inspire the free play of young imaginations. They grow up sensing that their ancestors and spirit-guides inhabit these stones, knowing that they are part of the flow of life from animal to plant to animal.

Hearing a tickety rattle, I turn my head slowly and open an eye. Five inches away from me is a bluntnose leopard lizard, *Gambelia silus*, like a gorgeous eleven-inch, four-footed jewel. Yellow stripes separate brown spots on his greenish gray body. His ethereal hands have long middle fingers that spread over the rock like digital wings. On his neck is a cluster of rusty garnets. For a moment's eternity, we stare at one another.

It is getting dark now, and I watch the rocks turn into buttocks, yoni, legs, knees, and water bowls. Still in my child-mind, I return to my camp and the late twentieth century.

Roadrunners etch the desert surface with nervous feet where lizards did push-ups during the heat of the day. I tilt my head back like a radar disk rotating toward the setting sun. A night hawk caws like chert hitting chert just before diving, then slices the air with his mechanical whir of wings. Where there were once melodic waterfalls of canyon wren, there are now insects sawing away in various frequencies like demented high-speed orchestras.

The Old Woman watches.

Petroglyphs pecked into Old Woman granite hundreds of years ago.

D riving forty miles north from the Old Woman Mountains, I arrive at the Mojave National Preserve. On a map it floats toward the west like the bow of a ship between Interstates 40 on the south and 15 on the north. Until 1995, there were no paved roads between these two major freeways, and visitors were those mavericks who like their wilderness experience raw and unfettered by services and explanatory signs.

Three of the four great American deserts converge here—the Sonoran, the Mojave, and the Great Basin. I have come in seach of the diverse flora and fauna, geology, and prehistoric sites which merge in the 1.4-million-acre preserve. Running through this newest unit of the National Park Service is the Mojave Road, an ancient Native American trail which ties together the human history of miners, ranchers, railroad and resort speculators, pioneers, tourists, and religious leaders, many of whom perished along this route. Even now, the complete Mojave Road can only be traveled by foot in places.

The Mojave Desert harbors bizarre volcanic features and pockets of extraordinary biodiversity and holds some of the most powerful sacred sites in the West. Some of these prehistoric sites are still in use, and the practices of shamanism and modern ethnobotany both merge here.

What I love about the Mojave Preserve is its camouflage: neither the infrequent, rough dirt roads nor the interstate scissor of I-40 and I-15 reveal its treasure. This is not a sit-on-your-butt-inside-your-car tourist haven, but a desert which demands stamina and a keen curiosity. I begin my exploration of the Mojave on its far western edge, in the mountains.

We Lose a River and Gain a Dune System

In the San Bernardino Mountains, a youthful Mojave River lurches, froths, roars, and leaps like a mountain lion.

The Mojave River Wash in Afton Canyon. The BLM has spent a great deal of effort and funds in Tamarisk removal here. Tamarisk, an invasive extoic from Africa, sucks up water and pushes out native plants.

Dry Lakes
and Lost Rivers

THE MOJAVE RIVER

I sleep by this fine, wild water in its granite vise, amid tall firs. The river's water, pure-smelling silk on the morning air, thunders me awake.

Seventy miles east, I go in search of this river again. Same river, no water—merely a great, wide sink, heat waves boiling the edges between the illusion of water and sand and dry air. Instead of a roaring mountain river, I find bone-dry Soda "Lake." Mojave "Wash." I am standing down in a graben, a gigantic fault basin whose sizzling alchemy swallows an entire river. The essence of the Mojave Desert is expressed in the word "sink." The water sinks downward into the earth or is sucked upward into the astringent, copper sky.

There is nothing so confounding to us temperate-climate humans than a disappearing river. Proper streams should drain into bigger streams, and then into bigger streams, then into rivers, then into oceans. In the basins of the Mojave Preserve, rivers sink into the bowels of the earth, leaving Demeter to weep over her hot saline sands. Her daughter Persephone was carried off to the underworld, and Demeter will not see plant life return until February. It will grow lush in March and April, then be gone by summer.

This is quintessential Mojave: dry lake beds surrounded by sharp mountains. Flat lake bottoms formed in land dropped down by faulting. As karsts, or blocks of metamorphic and igneous crust, rose upward, layers of sedimentary rock on their tops eroded and slid, creating a wall of sharp mountains all around. Over the millenia, erosion has built enormous fans of talus spreading out from these mountains into oval amphitheaters.

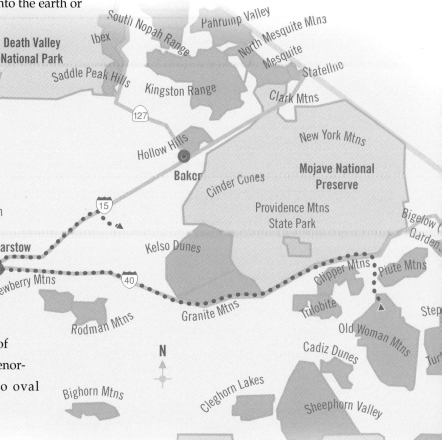

The Muck Stops Here

The once-deep, dip-slip fault valley bottoms are now filled with hundreds of feet of clay, salt, and fine particles from the surrounding mountains. Torrential floods wash salt and clay from the alluvial fans and flush them into the sinks. Flood water, rich with minerals, rapidly evaporates, causing salts and other chemicals to float to the top and crystallize.

The winter sun heats up. I spider-walk over Soda Lake's crunching sulphur-salt crystals spiking up in scalloped, pinnacled ridges. The water that does make it down into this basin bears arsenic, bicarbonate of soda, boron, calcium, chloride, magnesium, and potassium—chemical compounds very useful to mankind. Peering down at my boots, I imagine myself as a giant walking over the

Traveling east from Barstow, I enter the endless topography of the East Mojave. The Mojave Road carried Native Americans, settlers, miners, and religious seekers to their scattered destinations.

The austerity of Soda Lake and its surroundings offers stark beauty, while it confounds our temperate-climate sense of survival.

The Mojave—which includes the newly expanded Death Valley National Park, the Mojave National Preserve, and most of Joshua Tree National Park—is a strikingly beautiful Basin and Range province. An extensive grid of fault lines and tectonic plate movement have dropped the desert floor down, and pushed the mountains upward thousands of feet. In Death Valley, the lowest point in the United States, Badwater, at -282 feet, contrasts with the 11,049-foot Telescope Peak in the Panamint Range a few miles to the west. A great many plant and animal species are endemic only to the Mojave, although its northern border transitions into the Great Basin Desert just as its southern boundary merges with the Sonoran.

STILL WILD, ALWAYS WILD

The spines of a grizzly bear cactus, in the Mojave Desert, offer protection from the sun as well as from grazing animals.

crusty spine of the Rocky Mountains. Foot-high crystal ridges of rock-hard salts jag up rhythmically every two feet; they are blinding, shimmering white. In the distance, I observe a wide, shallow "lake." At 128 degrees, this mirage would be torturous to thirsty men.

Austerity creates its own startling beauties. All around the wide playa, volcanic shards in necks, mesas, and solitary peaks suggest fire. But I stand on a crystalline surface which looks like ice. To the east lies Devil's Playground—a sci-fi movie set at once hostile, jagged, and totally enticing. Formed by vulcanism in recent geological time, its perpendicular columns shoot straight eight hundred feet out of a lunar landscape. It is a lovely, eerie morning.

I enjoy imagining the first white explorers to trek across these dry, treacherous lands. Reading of their systematic search for a railroad route through the Southern California desert, I was surprised by the stubbornness of these men: with their temperate-climate, engineering logic, they were convinced that the Mojave River would lead them from the coastal mountains succinctly and economically down to the Colorado River on the Arizona border. From there, they were sure, a route along the Gila River could carry natural resources, such as gold and timber, from California across the country.

They were in for a shock.

One hundred and fifty years ago, government explorers were not armed with knowledge of desert geology nor with maps. On October 23, 1853, Lieutenant R. S. Williamson began following the Mojave River, searching for the easiest route across the desert to the mouth of the Gila River. In his notes from the expedition, the lieutenant wrote:

At Depot Camp [in the San Bernadino foothills] it was a broad, shallow stream, abundantly wooded, and its bottom confined by terraces on either bank, from one to three miles apart. The water, however, soon sank in the sandy bed . . . .

Upon emerging from the cañon, we entered a sandy plain, and at once lost all signs of the river-bed. After traveling 13 miles across this plain, we were fortunate enough to find a hole containing water, and here we made our camp late at night. The water was barely sufficient for our nearly exhausted animals, and a long time was occupied in giving them a scanty supply.

Still hopeful, Williamson eventually followed the river's dry wash southeast into low sand hills (the Kelso Dunes). Then he was thwarted and ended his expedition after reaching the dry lake bed now called Soda Lake—fifteen miles long and encrusted with bitter salts.

From high within Devil's Playground's southernmost mountains, I hear a familiar rumble. A silver passenger train speeds through from Los Angeles. Inside the cool protection of the double-glazed, air-conditioned train, passengers gaze or doze as they pass through bizarre mountains, brick red cinder cones, Joshua trees raising their schizoidal arms in yucca-spear prayers, giant lava tubes, petroglyphic shaman sites, limestone earth bowels with lacey secretions . . . on and on through earth's grand tumult of geology. The train passes as swiftly, as instantaneously, as a dream.

The beavertail cactus pads impersonate rock, while their blooms attempt to attract the universe.

I am driving down from Baker, California, late one afternoon when I spy a strange, rosy ocean in the distance. Ten miles off, soft sand waves lap toward granite mountains. Their leading edge stacks up 550 feet in a final crest, signaling a sudden decrease in wind velocity. Here, where wind has relinquished a treasure, a full forty-five square miles of sand are heaped up at the end of a wind funnel down the Mojave River Valley.

In these dunes, the mechanics of wind are diagrammed in the lyricism of sand.

The male wind and the female sand dance a lovely pas de deux in the later afternoon sun, which casts long, sensual shadows over the dunes. As in ballet, the dancers are soft and smooth from a distance, but all flesh and sweat up close. To know such dunes is to know my own sweat and muscles—I've got to climb them. I drive west two extremely bumpy miles and sleep at their base. The next morning, I find myself huffing and sweaty, backed into what little shade I can eke from white bursage halfway up the lee side of Kelso Dunes. It is spring, and the dunes are sprinkled with the bright reddish violet blooms of the endemic Borrego locoweed.

Like all dune systems, Kelso Dunes is rich in species found nowhere else on earth. This eastern Mojave dune system is as different from the Eureka Dunes as it is from the Algodones. Because species evolve within a particular set of dunes, diverging in form and DNA from similar species in another dune system—and because Kelso Dunes lie far from other dunes—a number of species are restricted to these few dozen square miles. Two unique scarab beetles, *Glaresis arenata* and *Aegialia kelsoi*—as well as newly discovered beetles, *Batuliodes*, and moths in the genus of *Onocnemis*—fly and creep through these glorious spring flowers.

Cow pies! I find cow plotzes all the way up the dunes. Ranchers still have grazing allotments across the Mojave, whether the vegetation can support the herds or not. What do cattle find to eat in this sparse vegetation?

The smaller cross-wave pattern on the large Cadiz Dunes seem echoed in the enormous forms of the surrounding mountains.

Pas de Deux/ Wind and Sand

KELSO DUNES

Most of this landscape is bare sand. Wandering stems of big galleta grass and Indian rice grass, however, do take hold here. Well adapted to unstabilized dunes, they send out long roots from which new grass springs. When these stems lie uncovered by the wind, they look like long tresses on the hills. Cattle dine up here on the big galleta grass and rice grass, as well as on Thurber's penstemon and cobweb phlox.

The herds pose a threat to the dunes' fragile plant life, which has also been ravaged by off-road vehicles. The BLM closed Kelso Dunes to ORVs in 1973, but twenty-three years later, the vegetation has not yet recovered from the crushing of plant and soil.

I squint upward at the looming Granite Mountains, which shoot straight up from the flat desert floor. These peaks, which look too craggy to climb without a rope, are the most critical element shaping Kelso Dunes. They trap the wind, forcing it to lift upward and drop the sand grains it carries in wave patterns.

To the east, the grand Providence Mountains sandwich white limestone against igneous rock and turn upward at a steep angle. The north end looks like the double bow of two ocean liners sinking. Some of the most unique cave formations on the planet snake through the limestone strata within these mountains, creating sacred spaces in which ancient shamans carried out their healing rituals. It is to them that I will go next.

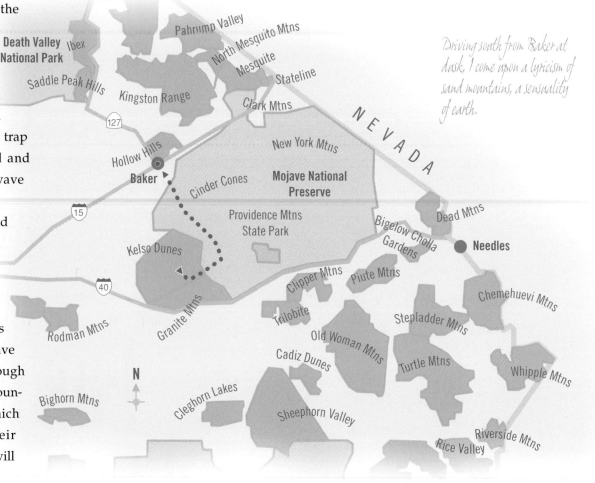

Driving south from Baker at dusk, I come upon a lyricism of sand mountains, a sensuality of earth.

The Granite Mountains at the south end of Mojave Wash force the wind to rise over them and drop their load of sand on Kelso Dunes.

DUNE FORMATION

Dunes are waves, just like sound waves or waves in the ocean, only infinitely slower. They are built by the multiplicity of minutia: each tiny grain is swirled on high by a valley's prevalent wind. When the wind must suddenly rise over a steep pass, it is forced to drop its load of sand grains precisely on the crest of the building dune. Soon the rising dunes themselves become an obstacle that slows the wind, and the grains of sand are dropped sooner and sooner, forming a precise pattern of smaller waves.

Dune borders shift relatively little. Because of the position of the mountains that surround them, wind forces persist in a predominate direction, blowing grains up the gentle side of the dune and dropping them down the steep face, moving the crests of sand minutely forward.

Dunes are of several kinds: barchan, star-shaped, transverse, and parabolic. Barchan dunes' sharp ends point away from the dominant wind direction, while transverse dunes form perpendicular to the predominant wind. Star-shaped dunes form where there are two or more wind directions. An arid land of barren soils, strong winds, and an abundant sand supply initiate transverse dunes. The sharp ends of horseshoe or parabolic dunes point into the wind where shrubs attach them to earth in shallower sand. They have massive, concave middles that curve away from the wind, forming baskets to catch more sand.

The moving front of the dune, the slipface, is always the steepest and, can be, almost perpendicular.

STILL WILD, ALWAYS WILD

Somewhere deep within the Mojave is a shaman's cave that holds the sunrise. It lies twenty-five feet up a solid granite monolith. A small triangular hole is cut clear through to the other side of the rock, framing a slice of sky. At first, my hopes of climbing inside are dashed: the front of the cave requires rock climbing skills. Around the back of this hundred-foot-high granite dome, I find stair steps up the crumbling rock. There seems to be no way in except through a tiny hole, until I discover I can shimmy over a hump near a steep drop-off onto an eastward balcony. A triangular entrance to the cave three feet above this reveals a highly polished stone floor the size of a dinner table.

Climbing cautiously into the cave, I find myself on slickrock which slopes toward the sheer cliff face. I am entranced by a wondrous array of fifty or more pictographs. Painted in deep reds, bright rust orange, white, and black, they emanate power from every surface except the floor. The most prominent, although its pigment is swiftly fading, is a 2-1/2-foot oval on the ceiling which has a series of concentric U-shaped forms surrounded by outwardly radiating lines. An archeologist has told me that such forms can symbolize a portal—a sacred passageway between two states of being, from the external world to an internal one, from the everyday world into the underworld, the world of the spirits. Caves themselves can symbolize the same concepts.

Overhead, an abstract figure of a bighorn sheep suggests a connection to the four song groups that embody healing ritual and storytelling among contemporary Chemehuevi people: the Salt Song, the Deer Song, the Mountain Sheep Song, and the Shaman or "Doctor" Song. A panel hidden behind the large back wall reveals concentric Vs inside an outline of the cave's profile. Under it, two lines with cross-hatches suggest that the prehistoric occupants had a ladder up the cliff face. Cautiously, I inch out toward the slick lip of the cave.

In a past time of harsh living conditions, birth was considered a great gift. Many centuries of women's knees polished Rebirth Rock deep in the Mojave Desert.

Solstice, Song, and Shaman

THE SUNRISING CAVE

Gazing back at the slice of sky framed by the opening through which I have climbed, I take out my compass and discover a clue to the powerful nature of this cave: the entrance faces due east and the large opening, westward. Directions are named in pairs according to the Chemehuevi, and east-west is the most sacred.

Although we cannot know the Ancients Ones who originally performed seasonal rituals here, we do know that as recently as seventy years ago the wise, elder men of the Chemehuevi were tracking the position of constellations in order to predict when spring began and when to plant. In a time before the advent of written calendars, this ability to predict spring must have been viewed as a remarkable, spiritual gift. Early anthropologists recorded the Chemehuevi stories of how the old men would come up out of their earth houses to stand naked in a predawn sky. Soon, however, as the young went to work for white men and learned to read their calendar, there was no one left to receive the ancient lore. The old men's knowledge perished upon their deaths.

In late afternoon, I curl up to sleep inside the cave, but the wind howls through. This hole through the granite is a wind funnel; wind is slowly carrying away the pigments of these mysterious paintings. What are we losing before we even understand?

How powerful astronomical observations must once have been, imbuing life with an orderly prediction of rotating seasons. All through the night, I dream of the cave from a safe bed in a more prosaic campsite. Above me, the solstice cave remains. It waits for the longest day of the year when the sunrise will align with its entrance, it waits for an old shaman to turn east and west on its floor.

To the Native American, natural rock forms hold potent meanings, and they are enhanced by petroglyphs.

STILL WILD, ALWAYS WILD

SHAMANS' CAVES

Many native people believe that a cave is a portal into another world.

The California desert is riddled with caves. They are created by wind, water, and earthquake, or are left gaping after land slumps out of softer layers of rock. Caves were greatly used by the first Americans for protection from harsh weather, living quarters, and storage of food, such as piñon nuts, grains, and acorns. Certain caves—especially those with particular shapes and sizes, multiple entrances, special compass directions, and relationships to the stars or sun—were held to be highly sacred by the Ancient Ones, as they still are by the Chemehuevi, the Cahuilla, and other contemporary tribes.

The first Americans believed, and still believe, that supernatural beings inhabit natural forms, particularly caves. These denizens are spirits who help with childbirth or fertility, demons who dwell inside of whirlwinds, and forces that cause the seasons to turn or lend datura its hallucinatory powers.

Some caves are solstice caves, their openings aligned with sunrise or sunset on the longest or shortest day of the year. Caves which have two or more openings, passageways through solid rock, or those hidden in dangerous or isolated places hold special power. Some caves and rock images are considered so sacred that a regular person should not lay eyes on them for fear of risking retaliation from angry spirits. Some are used for healing, the shaman chanting first to the west, then to the east, then to the west, until the source of the disease is found. Several particular stones, believed to be birthing rocks, have been polished by tens of thousands of Native American women kneeling to give birth.

In a cave, a man or woman may become a shaman by dreaming visions, hearing the songs that empower the tribe, or by hearing the voice of his spirit-animal, who will become his helper. However, a shaman must hear his sacred songs hundreds of times in order to know that his is a true calling, for shamanism is a lifelong journey demanding years of training and an ability to have and be open to visions and voices. It also means becoming a scientist of botany, medicine, and psychology, and building on an ancient, collective body of knowledge about the natural world and its relationships.

This information was gathered from The Chemehuevis, by Carobeth Laird, as well as from interviews with sources who wish not to be named.

I f the Cinder Cones are the Mojave's teenagers, brazen and energetic, its granite-and-limestone mountain ranges are its middle-aged poker players. To the casual driver on the main roads, such mountains appear in gray-patterned monotones. Their drab poker faces mumble, "Nothin' here . . . drive on . . . drive on." Yet camouflaged behind their gigantic stone slabs are canyons that sweep upward through four ecological zones. Their forested slopes are filled with springs, rock art, sacred sites, open-air historical museums, abandoned mines, and unique animal and plant species. Their highly fractured granite-and-limestone rock holds on to moisture, their soils are rich with diverse life, and their higher elevations are blanketed with thick juniper-piñon forests.

The New York and Clark Mountains of eastern California sit around the same plutonic table as the Old Woman and Piute Mountains to the south and the Kingston Range to the north—all vast, igneous fists of rock formed at great depth in the earth's crust and thrust upward. They are not part of the batholith of the Sierra Nevada.

Driving from the Cinder Cones southeast to the New York Mountains, I am filled with anticipation. I expect to find the Ol' Poker Face Mountains flush with life. The road goes up steeply through desert scrub, through a thick forest of multiarmed Joshua trees, *Yucca brevifolia jaegeriana*. Finally, at 5,470 feet, I reach camp, nestled under large desert-edge oak, *Quercus turbinella californica*, and lush piñon trees. This is incredibly dense vegetation for the Mojave Desert, and biologists have found an exceptional diversity of flowering plants here. Tomorrow I plan to climb toward the highest point in the East Mojave, New York Peak, a class-4 climb to 7,532 feet. I am in search of a refugium on its north slope, an Ice Age relict, of white firs, a conifer typical not of the desert but of the moist mountains of Oregon.

My climb begins on an old mining road which winds steeply up through granite boulders that, in

Granite boulders weather out of solid igneous rock in the New York Mountains.

Requiem for an Ice Age

CINDER CONES AND THE NEW YORK MOUNTAINS

some places, now block the way. When I reach the abandoned shafts, I drop into a creek bottom which is covered with polished limestone and marble cobble eroded from the 250- to 300-million-year-old Permian limestone at the top of this drainage. The many trickles that converge here in a stream have carved the limestone into a bowl as white as porcelain and two miles across.

I look up, daunted. The wall of the mountain is fairly vertical and covered with monoliths the size of New Jersey. I begin to boulder scramble, a climbing technique using all four limbs but not a rope. I keep looking back down to retrace my route and find, anxiously, that it appears to drop away into infinity.

Finally, I sit at the base of a peak shaped like five-hundred-foot stone dolphins leaping straight up in the air. I feel dizzy with the height of it all and dwarfed by the mountain's immensity. I had forgotten the spine-zinging thrill of peak climbing. All around me skeletons of piñon twist their death-angst against an impossibly blue sky. The clouds whirl by the peak in time-lapse motion. I am chilled to the bone and thrilled to the core.

After resting, I make my way around to the north side of the peak—and find no refugium. I realize suddenly that New York Peak is still another ridge and three more miles away. I cannot reach the refugium in one day. As it is, down-climbing the way I came will be tedious, if not dangerous—dark shadows already slide over my route up.

A red-tail hawk sweeps around a corner five feet away from my chest, so close that I can hear the distinct whir of each flight feather as she sheers by. The panorama is so vast I can take in 300 degrees, two hundred miles, and two or three states—up into the Great Basin, down into the Sonoran Desert, and far north to Death Valley. To the south, the Piute and Old Woman Ranges are aligned with one another. East-northeast, the Castle Mountains lie sacrificed to gold hunger and cyanide like so many pink and white layers of ersatz cake. To the north-northeast, I see the slim dorsal fin of Cathedral Peaks, and to the north, the Kingstons' long ridge rises six thousand feet above the desert floor like a blue tidal wave. There lies another refugium, isolated by sixty miles from its nearby genetic cousin in the New York Mountains.

Reluctantly, I head down the way I came. The down-climb leaves my legs covered with long stripes of blood from stiff blue yucca and scrub oak. Three hours later, back in camp, I am grateful for the huge, cool piñons and oaks which arch over me like cloisters. All evening, a flammulated owl calls: *hoooo . . . hoooo . . . hooo . . . hooo. . . .*

Four types of rock are juxtaposed in the Mojave Preseve: volcanic, in the Cinder Cones; igneous, in the granite New York Mountains; sedimentary, in the limestone layers of the Providence and New York Mountains; and metamorphic, also in the New York and Providence Mountains, where heat and pressure have transformed the limestone and granite into metamorphic rock.

The Nopah Mountains
Wilderness is part of the Lost
Triangle between Death Valley
National Park and East
Mojave. "Pah" means water—
there is no water here.

REFUGIUM

 relict plant community, called a refugium, is an ecological remnant of an earlier age during which precipitation and temperatures were quite different. A refugium survives in microclimates similar to the earlier climatic conditions, such as the wet north slopes of desert mountains or certain sunny, dry hills of central Alaska which were unscraped by glaciers.

In the California desert, small patches of closed-cone pines, which grew during the last ice age twenty thousand years ago, are now relegated to a few maritime and inland sites in which summer and winter temperatures are moderated by the sea or a deep canyon. White fir and limber pine, which now grow on moist slopes of mountain elevations in just a few desert places, were once part of a continuous forest from mountain range to mountain range across much of California. The white fir once grew in all the Mojave mountains. Now only isolated forests

The Clark Mountains hold a refugium left over from the last ice age. Refugia are botanical treasure chests which give ecologists important clues into the desert's continuum of life.

survive in desert canyons in the New York, Clark, and Kingston Mountains. These remnant plants struggle within narrow parameters of existence set by climate, disease, and competition with newer, desert-adapted species.

Because these older plants carry DNA that may be long gone in surrounding areas, they are a genetic resource that can be tapped when needed in the future. When the climate again shifts—and climate is always changing—plants preserved in a refugium, already adapted to similar condi-tions, can repopulate devastated habitats.

A prime example of the importance of a refugium exists within the Southern California desert itself. The Sonoran Desert was once a wetter, colder chaparral. When it changed rapidly to desert ten to twelve thousand years ago, it was able to repopulate itself with desert-adapted plants from species preserved in a refugium in Mexico.

THE YOUNG AND THE EXPLOSIVE

An early morning walk over a tall ridge of bulbous black rock in the Cinder Cones of the Mojave Preserve reveals a land born yesterday. Brilliant chartreuse, orange, and yellow lichens stand out against its ropey, metallic surface.

I scramble over slabs of glassy lava and bomb-shaped clinkers, blobs of hot lava which cooled as they flew through the air. The surfaces are outrageous, from bubbly to conchoidally fractured with beautiful scallop-shaped concavities, and filled with basket-ball-sized to microscopic gas holes. When it is pure, the silicate in the lava becomes obsidian, ideal for arrow points and cutting tools. Lava tubes one hundred feet high shine like heavy iron just poured out of the caster's forge. In summer, heat pulsing off these hulks could fry an egg or my flesh in minutes.

I sit at the base of Aiken Cone, a perfect red triangle rising eight hundred feet in the air. The water source at its base attracts hundreds of birds! All around me, birds coo, croak, croon, quibble, chortle, and court: roadrunner, quail, house finch, mockingbird, and shrike. Above, the square-winged silhouette of a golden eagle spirals up the air thermals.

These youthful volcanoes, which lie scattered from Baker almost to Los Angeles, may be as young as one hundred thousand years old. Even though they are short-lived and less dangerous than the more massive volcanoes of the Pacific Northwest, they are unpredictable. It is a great mystery why these cones appear where they do; they are not connected to any single fault system and cannot be explained by a subduction zone such as the one along the Pacific Rim. There are no theories about the timing or the placement of their eruptions. They are capable of sprouting up wherever they please—through a nuclear waste site, through Las Vegas, or through a sandy arroyo, such as here—always with spectacular fireworks.

I drive the mile to the top of Aiken Cone, where the wind howls melodrama-style. Cinder cones are formed of tephra, or hole-pierced rock of uniform size and surprisingly light weight, which the cone spewed out along with ash, pumice, and the spherical bombs of molten lava. When the cone plugged its own vent, viscous lava breached the weakest side and flowed out the cone's base in a tube for miles.

Now, at sunset, the intense yellow brittlebush against the black or red rock suggests the fiery pyrotechnics from which the cones are born. I fall to sleep with a full, orange moon rising over a red horizon.

The 209,608 acres of the Kingston Range Wilderness acts as a huge, triangular joint which connects the Mojave, the Sonoran, and the lower Great Basin Deserts. Kingston Peak is a crazy quilt of ecosystems, more than five hundred flowering plants in a twenty-by-thirty-mile space. It is one of the most botanically diverse wildernesses in the California desert, ranging from riparian wash to high mountain crag in a matter of miles. As in the New York Mountains, there is a refugium of white fir on the northern slope of Kingston Peak, which, at 7,323 feet, rises like an ecological island from the desert floor. From seventeen miles of continuous ridgeline above 6,000 feet, an elegant alluvial slope, a *bajada*, sweeps down to Kingston Wash. As I drove here from the New York Mountains fifty miles south, I watched the *bajada*, sidelit by an orange sun, transform into a green quilt. Each puckered thread line indicated the sinuous curve of an arroyo. Below lay Kingston Wash, a year-round wetland and a diverse habitat for birds, fish, mammals, reptiles, and insects.

Now, it is night. I am on a hunting safari. Unlike Hemingway, my weapons are a head lamp and a guidebook. Very much unlike Hemingway's game, the giants of the African Savannah, my saurian quarry is only three inches long. I search rock ledges of the Kingston Range for the western banded gecko, *Coleonyx variegatus*.

Geckos are an extended family of tropical lizards who communicate by chirping to one another. Their round toes are covered with numerous villi, microscopic hairs with spatula-shaped ends that cling to any surface. They run up walls, across ceilings, or over smooth rock faces with the greatest of ease. Their vertical pupils, typical of many night creatures, and flesh-colored skin camouflaged by bands and dots create handsome, if somewhat invisible, critters. I'm very frustrated.

I have been climbing for an hour now and look down to discover three hundred feet of craggy rock

Storms in the desert are glorious displays of power, light, and sudden downpours.

Of Barefoot Geckos and Unbridled Lilies

THE KINGSTON MOUNTAINS

below me. Alas, no gecko. I can see the lights of Las Vegas searing the eastern skyline. I begin scrambling down rough, red, granitic slabs, the core of the Kingstons. My head has been down, searching for that illusive night-stalker as he hunts insects in the rocky terrain.

But it does not pay to be so single-minded when searching in the desert. There are many other treasures to be found. Under the floodlight of a half moon, fifteen-foot flower stalks of *Nolina parryi* glow on the flanks of Kingston Peak. Three other members of the lily family, the Mojave yucca, the blue yucca, and the Joshua tree, variation *jaegeriana*, also glow at night when they are blooming. The nolina, often mistaken for yucca, has a barrel of narrow, flexible, sword-shaped leaves, each four feet long. Nolina ghosts are surreal white cylinders in the moonlight.

The nolina bloom, I believe, was invented by the moon. In its cool, reflected light, hundreds of papery white plumes stretch out all around the nolina's central pole, luminous. Moths are drawn to that ghostly, reflected flower-light; thus the yucca and nolina attract their pollinators and ensure their survival.

Nolinas are most commonly found above the Salton Sea in the Chuckwalla, Orocopia, and Old Woman wildernesses and in Joshua Tree National Park. Although this is the northernmost range of nolina habitat, the plants here do not peter out: these are outstanding specimens, both in size and elegance.

I drove north from the New York to the Kingston Mountains in search of the biodiversity and the illusive refugia.

From the New York to the Kingston Range, an exceptional species, the *jaegeriana* Joshua tree, jazzes the skyline as if its startling poses were choreographed by Martha Graham herself. The tree's short-leaved, bottle-brush-like, multiple arms give it a frenzied look in the night. Although it also graces I-15 between Baker and Las Vegas, it is on the Kingstons that this Joshua tree seems most at home. Over twenty-five species of birds build their nests in its fluid arms; the Navajo yucca borer butterfly, the night lizard, beetles, and moths call this plant dinner, shelter, and home.

Still no gecko. From probing the earth, I look upward. There! At the zenith is a huge disk of light with a long, wide tail glowing in three dimensions. I catch my breath. Hyakutake! The comet, with a six- to ten-mile diameter hunk of rock and ice, trails in a wide arc across the heavens.

In deserts, beauty is never what you have dreamed or planned. The next morning, I am up early. There—right on the road in front of me—is a flesh-colored twig. A gecko!

Parry's nolina flower stalks stand twelve feet high in the Kingston Mountains.

It is mid-December. Snow is falling on a red rock wall six hundred feet high. I have entered a kingdom of bubble-gum pink tuff-breccia, brilliant red sandstone, red orange cross-bedded conglomerate, and bone white volcanic ash. All these layers are weathered into the shapes of bishop's hats, Greek statues, organ pipes, and many-windowed condominiums. The harder red sandstone layers jut out like balconies, catching the snow. The soft white ash layers are more hole than rock. Snow is transforming the red stone into high-contrast beauty.

Such surreal magnificence—where have I seen it before? I've seen it behind Ronald Reagan in *Death Valley Days*. Under the "terrible lizards" in *Jurassic Park*. As the home of furry actors in *Beneath the Planet of the Apes*. In the *Flash Gordon* series and television's *Duel in the Desert*. So much film as been exposed to the Ricardo formation here that its dazzling red oxides lie deep within the American psyche, charged with emotion. It is not a rational landscape; it embodies the West and the American Myth.

In spring, the arroyos and hills here are flush with more than two hundred flowering plants, among them rare endemics such as the fish hook cactus, Red Rock Canyon tarweed, and spiny chorizanthe. Because of the worldwide uniqueness of the area's rock formations and plant species, the BLM recently added 20,500 acres to the jurisdiction of Red Rock Canyon State Park. After subtracting inholdings and mining claims, the new wilderness area is nearly 18,500 acres.

Two adjacent areas on the western border of the park, Dove Springs and Jawbone Canyons, have been sacrificed to off-road vehicle use, so there are still many acres of death-defyingly steep mounds on which drivers can test their engines and testosterone. Although the soft hills next to the most spectacular red cliffs have been off-limits to ORVs for twenty years, there are still scarred, wide strips of vegetation missing. It will

Volcanic ash and pink tuff create the outlandish hues around Red Rock Canyon.

Where Major Faults Intersect

RED ROCK CANYON

take another generation for the ecosystem to recover.

It takes only one fault system in an area to jumble desert geology into a tumult of beauty, and at Red Rock, within a very small area, three major faults converge. The Garlock fault, which runs all the way through south Death Valley, and its parallel fault, the El Paso, butt into the Sierra Frontal fault. The Garlock has a showdown with the Sierra Frontal fault, and the resulting shootout is blood red escarpments and wild topography.

Along these major fault escarpments, the topography shifts from the gentle basins and promontories of the preserve into the dramatic Basin and Range topography of Death Valley. Here, fossils stretching in age from the Precambrian era, 2.5 to 4.5 billion years ago, up to recent time, converge in a multi-ticolored array of outrageous geological features.

In the spring, I drive down into Last Chance Canyon, which drains the western flanks of the El Paso Mountain Wilderness and connects the state park with the El Paso Mountains. A pack of survivalists is rumored to live somewhere up in this black volcanic range, where they have amassed an arsenal of high-powered weapons. I do not verify this for myself.

Last Chance Canyon cuts through the Ricardo and the Garlock formations, bright red layers interspersed with black basaltic flows. The basalt weathers into elegant mushroom-shaped mesas because the darker caprock of andesite-basalt protects the more rapidly eroding layers underneath.

On the back of a huge boulder of colorful breccia, I find two pictographs in iron oxide: a figure suggesting a rain cloud and two figures side by side. Last Chance, Nightmare, and Mesquite Canyons, with their nesting golden eagles and abundant wildlife, were very sacred to the original Americans who lived here.

This was also a major passage from the interior to the coast and a trading center until early this century. The indigenous people, the Kawailsu and the Tehachapi, had and still have permanent

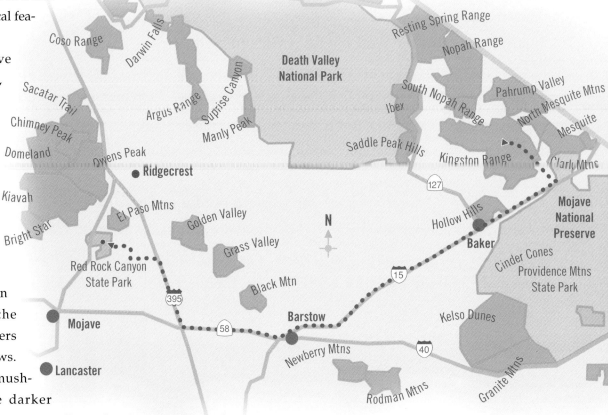

Red Rock Canyon State Park and the El Paso Mountains mark the transition from the lower Mojave into the Basin and Range Mojave of Death Valley National Park.

Riparian habitat in Last Chance Canyon in Red Rock Canyon State Park.

In graben and karst topography, the graben block with faults on both sides slip downward, while the karsts slide upward and erode into the mountain ranges we see today.

THROUGH EVERY FAULT
OF OUR OWN

The outer crust of the earth is in constant motion. Tectonic plates move like thick skin on the surface of a boiling pudding, constantly churning around in vertical loops and remelting within the asthenosphere, a plastic layer of the earth's crust. Volcanoes, earthquakes, faulting, and warping result from the slow-motion smashing of the earth's crustal fragments.

One of the most seismically active areas on the entire globe is Southern California. It is at once blessed and cursed with multiple cracks in the continental plate. If these cracks do not move, they are called joints. If, however, the rock on either side does move, the cracks become faults. Faults build up tension. They are held in place by pressure and friction, until one day they release and slide suddenly from side to side or up and down, or both.

California's most notorious fault, the San Andreas, runs 660 miles from Mexico to Mendocino and is highly active. Over the millennia, it has moved hundred of miles. There are thousands of fault lines running parallel or obliquely perpendicular to the San Andreas, such as the Blue fault and the Garlock fault.

Just as it can bring great tragedy where it passes beneath population centers, California's famous fault system creates the tremendous beauty of steep escarpments, hot and cold springs, sudden uplifts or down-drops of the earth's crust—the dramatic extremes of the Basin and Range topography.

and seasonal villages close by. For thousands of years, successive cultures have left behind their tools and arrow points, finely crafted from the chert found in wide lenses of rock nearby in the El Paso Mountains and throughout these canyons. These ancient inhabitants are called the Elko Springs People (2000 B.C. to 500 A.D.) and the Rose Spring People (500 to 1200 A.D.) by archeologists, who are making many exciting discoveries on the land newly added to the state park.

There are miles of backcountry roads leading throughout the bizarre red formations of the canyons. I decide I will camp here tonight, but while I am identifying birds, twenty-three dirt bikers roar down the canyon, right over the bright orange "Wilderness Closed" marker, and up over the fragile plants clinging to a steep, steep mountain slope. Their neon, color-coordinated outfits and designer mosquito-machines identify them as urbanites with extra money and no brains.

The dust banners from their plant-ripping tires wave hundreds of feet into the air, and the quiet of the canyon is shattered. I walk after them on foot, grumbling to myself: these urban renegades are the very idiots who destroy the freedoms of all four-wheelers, including ORV drivers who do obey the laws.

Instantly the area had become a One-Use Wilderness—their dirt and noise is incompatable with folks in Jeeps, legal dune buggies, and on foot or for the wildlife for miles around. Although it is potentially dangerous, I shake my long hair loose from under my hat and stride over to them to let them know that their behavior ruins the area for everybody else.

"In your face," they yell at me. "We are OUTLAWS!"

I awoke this morning on an African Savannah. Or at least that's what it felt like, with forty tall ears rotating like pointy satellite dishes above the sea of creosote and rabbit brush. One by one, burros appeared, handsome animals with dark gray to black velvet coats and white underbellies and muzzles, tails switching nervously.

At first, I forgot where I had slept. I had driven up North Death Valley Road at midnight into the new wilderness area added to the north of the national park. As the valley followed along the Last Chance fault line, spring after spring was marked by deep green foliage in the alluvial foothills.

In the 1920s, Sand Spring had a gas station and store to supply the Skookum mines. This morning, however, all I find is wind and an empty trench filled with Coleman and Bluet stove gas cans. Not even a foundation. Nearby, the stark skeleton of a cottonwood, all its limbs sheared off and bifurcated near the top, looks like a human supplicating heaven. To the west, the Last Chance Mountains loom, dark gray and menacing, their early Paleozoic sedimentary rocks capped by very young basalt. Sandy Peak rises from the desert floor to 7,062 feet.

Tall green reeds reflect perfectly down into a green water hole. Cottontails and iridescent female red-wing blackbirds constantly flit among the shrubs, and a dusky sparrow sings sweetly of water. A coyote twenty-five feet off examines me, unafraid for so long that I grow impatient. He is an extremely healthy animal of all shades of brown, red, and tan. I sing to him, and instead of moving, he rotates his ears forward to listen.

I travel north up the fault scarp, past soft white mounds of deeply eroded alluvial debris from the mountains. There have been no earthquakes in recent geological history in this highly volcanic area, and I pass by steep slopes of precarious boulders. At a folk art sculpture made of old crankshafts, I turn off to drive toward

Last Chance Spring supports bighorn sheep, fox, coyote, mountain lion, and hundreds of bird and insect species.

Springs Eternalize Hope

SAND SPRING AND LAST CHANCE SPRING

Last Chance Spring. The washed-out, rocky road climbs steeply and steadily, and finally I spy a lush stand of trees, a sign of water.

Spreading out gear to set up camp at an abandoned tin cabin with a rusted stove pipe, two hundred yards from the spring, I debate whether to sleep closer to the water. But this is close enough: it is not good to frighten animals from their only drinking source. Where cattle have trailed back and forth to a water tank, the ground is ruined, but the surrounding shrub is lush and dense. I just don't grasp the urge to bring huge, nonindigenous ungulates into a land that can barely support wide-roving deer and sheep herds. On up the canyon, mine shafts plunge down at 60 degrees with rickety wooden structures above them. In the colorful tumult of igneous belch, I recognize precious mineral ores.

Farther up canyon lies something far more valuable than silver or gold. A huge walnut tree, as grand as any I have ever seen, is draped generously with wild grape, the leaves turning all shades of red and gold. Nearby, water seeps from the fragmenting rock cliff, water which rises from deep within the earth through a fault line. The trough pours off a gallon every two minutes.

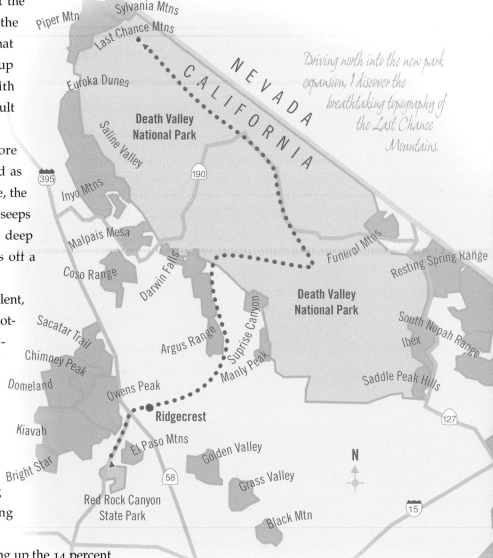

Driving north into the new park expansion, I discover the breathtaking topography of the Last Chance Mountains.

And what life! Suddenly, instead of the silent, dry desert floor of cholla, black bush, desert trumpet, and cottontop cactus, there is a constant burring, buzzing, chipping, chiming, singing, calling, chortling, and burbling. Through the lush piñon trees, a Scott's oriole, *Icterus parisorum*, flashes his deep yellow-orange sides and jet black head. The electric blue flashes of scrub jays weave the sky into the trees. A Mojave fringe-toed lizard dives by with brilliant rust spots near his eyes. *Ephedra*, Mormon tea, is verdant up here. Painted ladies, pearly marble wing butterflies, and buzzing grasshoppers set the crumbling mountain talus aglow.

As I look up the slope, I think about walking up the 14 percent grade, then decide that I must fuel my body before beginning to climb the 7,000-foot peak.

It is one of the best decisions I ever made.

I sit within a perfect blind, my truck's canopy. As a mess of vegetables, eggs, and cheese is cooking, the ravens grow frantic and vocal. There! Just two hundred yards away up the damp, steep

BIGHORN SHEEP
OVIS CANADENSIS

Bighorn sheep, which once inhabited most of the wild desert mountain ranges, now live only in areas undisturbed by humans, wild burros, or domesticated animals. They in no way resemble their domestic counterparts: they are much larger, more muscular, and have coarse brown hair that reveals the shape of their bodies. Bighorns roam the barren mountain crags, feeding actively by day and watering in early morning and late afternoon at widely spaced desert springs. Because they receive a good deal of their moisture from their food, they water as infrequently as every two weeks in fall and winter. They can more easily be spotted in the hottest weeks of summer when they are forced to descend farther into the desert to rapidly disappearing water holes.

Rams average about five feet in length and three and a half feet in height, and weigh 160 to 200 pounds, depending on the location and availability of food. Generally the bighorn in Death Valley mate between late August and October, and a ewe gives birth to one lamb in March or April, although the timing for specific herds varies greatly depending on habitat. A typical herd of between twelve and twenty sheep will produce one or two lambs per year because of the harshness of the environment. The ewes separate themselves from the herd to give birth in order to give predators less chance to attack a cluster of newborns. The lambs are very soon on their feet and following their mothers swiftly over precipitous mountainsides which would be a challenge for human mountain climbers.

Photo by B. Moose Peterson

Still Wild, Always Wild

Darwin Falls in the Argus Mountains, a short walk from the road's end, is a deep, cool oasis in a dry desert canyon.

A desert spiny lizard in the Mojave.

AMERICA'S LARGEST WILDERNESS PARK OUTSIDE ALASKA: DEATH VALLEY NATIONAL PARK

On October 31, 1994, Death Valley National Monument was established as a national park, and its protection of the Mojave Desert was expanded from 2 million acres to over 3.3 million acres. In my brief experience of the spectacular new wilderness lands, I was overwhelmed by the unbounded opportunities for back-country hiking, backpacking, and exploring miles of paved and dirt roads in some of the wildest topography left on earth. These lands are a significant addition not only to America's heritage but to the world's. In 1984 Death Valley National Monument was recognized by the United Nations as a globally significant bioregion. As part of the Mojave and Colorado Deserts Biosphere Preserve, the park encompasses the extremes of Basin and Range, moving from 282 feet below sea level, the lowest elevation, to the 11,049-foot Telescope Peak, within tweny miles.

Within the newly protected wilderness boundaries are many endemic plants, as well as valuable fossils preserved over a period of six hundred million years, archeological treasures—giant stone alignments large enough to be seen from the air, and thousands of rock art and village sites.

The new wilderness boundaries protect many more ghost towns, ranches, and mining sites—such as Panamint City up Surprise Canyon—from inevitable destruction. One can stumble upon a ghost town complete with dishes, machinery parts, and bed frames, as if it were an open-air museum.

Although there are still mining inholdings and grazing allotments, 95 percent of Death Valley National Park is officially protected as wilderness. Much of the new boundary has yet to be surveyed, since it follows high mountain ridgelines in order to encompass complete ecosystems. The Greenwater Valley and Range to the east add on 150,000 new acres, while the isolated and magnificent Saline Valley adds 400,000 acres.

Death Valley's long-term wilderness plan now emphasizes the protection of desert lands for future generations rather than the development of more roads and concessions. Nonessential roads will be allowed, gradually, to return to nature, while more than two hundred miles of open roads within the old monument boundaries alone continue to lead into remote and surprising wilderness. For instance, only a half-mile walk from the end of the road, Darwin Falls transforms the dry desert floor into a lush, cool, riparian habitat of ferns, algae, moss, birds, and mammals—with the magnificent sound of pounding water. If I had fifty years and sturdy vehicles, I could still barely scratch the huge expanse of wilderness accessible by road. That sense of infinite wilderness is as sweet as the sound of desert water flowing.

slope are twelve of the most perfect bighorn sheep that could possibly be. Seeing them at such close range is very unusual; they are seldom found in the presence of humans. Even though they have been protected since 1883, poaching and encroachment on their habitat by humans, cows, and wild burros have diminished their numbers.

Full, muscular, well-fed, the herd files after the majestic ram. Normally he would not be with this group of ewes, but it is still close to mating season. His horns spiral around in a complete circle and would be over two feet long if unwound. They rise from the front of his head as bony, hollow *os cornu*, made up of a series of sheaths of hard epidermis. Although these magnificent cones are not shed, they are worn down steadily by being rubbed against rocks and bushes and other rams' horns during their ritualized battles. The females' horns are more demure and sweep up and backward.

What amazes me is the complete cooperation of the individual sheep with no apparent sounds or gestures between them. There is always one designated "watch sheep" whose head is up and alert while the rest eat. This one watches me intently, but does not seem disturbed, even when I stir my eggs. I am extremely careful in my movements, so as not to startle the sheep or force them to flee. Each time you cause a wild animal to change behavior and expend her energy unnecessarily, you cost her valuable calories. For an animal on the edge of existence, these few reserves could mean the difference between life and death. With mining encroaching on their territory, in this extremely dry year, these sheep will need all the calories they can glean.

I am so glad that I did not camp closer to the spring! I might have kept the sheep from their rare water supply. Because of their desert-adapted biology, they only need to drink once every two weeks in the fall and winter. Much of their moisture comes from their food. They drink under a huge piñon for a half hour, then come around a bluff only 130 yards away. The ewe moves the herd in twenty-minute intervals, never overgrazing any one spot, tasting a variety of vegetation. I feel so honored to be in their presence for two and a half hours—most of the time bighorn stay high above the desert plain in almost waterless rocky crags. They will not water where wild burros, who foul the springs, have been. In fact, wild burros, an exotic from Africa, wipe out the bighorn's food source and have decimated whole herds.

Suddenly, a stone clatters down a nearby bluff, and the sheep bunch together in fright; the ram, apart from the herd, stands up on a high rock like a Walt Disney character. His dark fleece contrasts dramatically with the light stone. After he steps down, a young ram mimics exactly his watchful stance.

When the sheep depart, they move as one animal with forty-eight legs and twenty-four eyes. Their off-white rumps form a handsome pattern, visible from far away.

Ibex Hills from Ibex Peak, a wilderness addition on the southeastern edge of Death Valley National Park.

To reach Eureka Dunes from Last Chance Spring, I drive over one of the most dramatic humps of sea sediment and vulcanism in the California desert—the Last Chance Mountains. Rising swiftly up to a 5,700-foot pass, the road crests on top of glassy black volcanic layers.

This is a surreal landscape of craters. Pimples. Ridges. Spiny fins. Paleozoic rock layers shoot up, 5 degrees off of perpendicular in pink, white, brilliant green, lavender, purple, red, black, and rust, juxtaposed with pit mines and bleak red volcanoes. The Last Chance Mountains produce sulphur, uranium, and mercury in active mines.

I plunge down the mountains' west side through the split Hanging Rock Canyon. I get my first sight of Eureka Valley and the steep Inyo Mountains, the new westward expansion of Death Valley. In the low, slanting sun, I see the western slope of the Last Chance Mountains.

My heart pauses. My mind can explain what I am seeing as Cambrian and Ordivocian sea sediments laid down 438 to 570 million years ago—but I'd rather just wander, wordless, in the lilac, chestnut, eggshell, cordovan, and purple glory of it all.

* * *

Now, as I gaze down on the huge sand mountains of Eureka Dunes, the sun creeps toward the top edge of the Last Chance Range, and the low-angle light plays F-stop hopscotch with the light and dark patterns in Eureka Valley. Ansel Adams, I imagine, not only rolls over, but sits up and salutes at what happens next: The mountains are damping toward black, the sky is hushing, the low, flat playa is closing down in desert dusk. The light is sucked toward the 690-foot-tall sand dunes in the distance at the southeast end of Eureka Valley. I can hear it rush past my ears like angels' wings.

A dormant shrub on Eureka Dunes, Death Valley National Park.

The Wind Made Visible

EUREKA DUNES AND EUREKA VALLEY

The huge sand mountains are lighter than anything else in the startling dark. It is twenty minutes before sundown, and the dunes are growing more luminous by the moment. Their central peaks are stunning triangles, while the left end lumps toward me in a series of lyrical pits and peaks that would make Brancusi weep.

There is the counter-intuitive thrill of seeing that part of the earth is far lighter than sky. To watch these dunes leap forward from their dark backdrop is to be lifted straight up from my own earthbound mind. My awe comes not merely from their large size but from the double-edged sword of fear and elation. Tomorrow I will be on their crest: How dangerous will it be? Will the sand catch and hold me? Will it sing, groan, or whisper as it buries me?

The Eureka Dunes

These dunes start at 2,900 feet and rise to higher that 3,600 feet. Their base is only three square miles, compared with the forty-five square miles of Kelso Dunes or the thirty-one square miles of Death Valley Dunes. Their granular gold sand comes from a Pleistocene lake bottom which dried up thousands of years ago. That sediment, in turn, was eroded from a mountain range which itself was formed of sediments washing down into an even more ancient, shallow ocean.

Biologically, dunes function as isolated sand islands in the sea of desert geography. Cut off by some sort of moat, in this case, high mountains and salt playas, this island harbors a genetic treasure: an endemic grain, the Eureka dune grass, *Swallenia alexandrae*, grows only in this one place on the entire globe. The unique DNA of this Eureka Dunes species could be used to save our American grain crops in case of an epidemic disease. Before the BLM closed the dunes to ORVs in 1976, the world almost lost it forever.

It is night—the stars cast their net of mythological beings across the universe. No wind. Every muscle fiber in my body is relaxing.

Suddenly, a blinding flash and a sharp cracking explosion deafens my ears and reverberates through the desert night from mountain to mountain for a full two minutes. I think about death and nuclear explosions and wonder what on earth has taken place in the world since I left news reports behind. After adrenaline stops zinging my limbs, I realize that these are military flares and explosions intentionally set off at night so as not to ruin the nerves of civilian visitors. Like me.

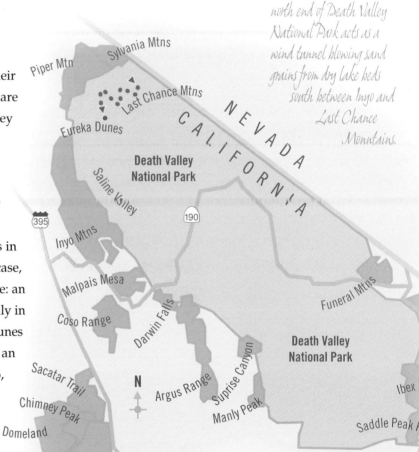

The Eureka Valley in the north end of Death Valley National Park acts as a wind tunnel blowing sand grains from dry lake beds south between Inyo and Last Chance Mountains.

Intense hues in rock layers at the Last Chance Pass.

Still Wild, Always Wild

The endemic Eureka dune grass survives in the shifting sands by the extension of its underground stems.

At dawn, last night's flares forgotten, I can hardly believe my eyes. The dunes are turning into liquid ivory and rising like giant tsunamis in front of me in austere silhouette. Their sinuous inner curves slowly distinguish themselves, one by one. The hummocks of plants, of endemic shiny locoweed and Eureka dune grass, arrowhead, and pleated coldenia cast exaggerated, pointed purple shadows. At the margins of the dunes, prince's plume, rice grass, hoary dictoria, and thorny dalea are gray winter skeletons. The rusts and golds of shadscale and fourwing saltbushes pluck themselves up from the soup of desert playa.

The temperature leaps from 30 to 73 degrees in less than an hour. Suddenly, there is a monstrous vibration in the ground, and all the birds rise straight up into the air. Around the east side of the dunes from a deep, narrow valley comes an Air Force trainer jet, absolutely silent until it is right upon me. Like the owl, its incredible engineering of ailerons (flaps) and wings make it deadly quiet. A moment later, its sound follows it like many tin cans on a rope, only a thousand times louder.

I don't know about the rest of the fauna out here, but I vote for the sacredness of wilderness air waves.

Sand dunes are permanent eddies and movable mountains. I start climbing. Every muscle in my legs aches and strains against the steep slope. Two-thirds of the way up, moving sideways across a dangerously steep slope like a spider, I collapse in the sand. This is hard work. There, below me, are the trailing stems of *Swallenia*. The only dune grass with its genes on the planet.

There is silence as I begin to come straight down from a dune crest, but soon a big sound, like a passenger jet engine, sometimes soft and sometimes quite loud, engulfs me. Guidebooks claim that scientists do not yet understand what makes dunes sing, but I feel the explanation in my legs and feet and heart. It is wave theory all over again—the same thing which causes pendulums in the same room to begin to swing in unison. This singing is the exact alignment of all the tiny sound waves into synchronistic crests and troughs which grow louder and louder.

I am plunging now, in a hurry to reach home (truck) and hearth (butane stove). In the evening light, however, something brings me to my knees. There in the sand is the rare, endemic dune evening primrose, *Oenothera deltoides*, not yet in bloom. I recognize it by its bird cage of dried branches which sweep upward in a sphere to protect the new growth. These Eureka endemics have evolved their unique strategies in an environment where survival is nearly impossible. I gaze out over the dark ring of mountains surrounding Eureka Valley. A golden haze coming from the north is undoubtedly bringing more sand. At once stark and frightening and magnificently awe-inspiring, this landscape attempts to bury and erase me with blowing grains.

DESERT TORTOISE
XEROPHERIC AGASSIZZII

Gazing head-on into the passive face of a desert tortoise shatters a number of my stereotypes. I am struck by how keenly he notices everything around him, how quickly he moves, and how handsome a creature he is.

The life of the tortoise, one of the longest-living animals on the planet, is passed in slow motion in a harsh environment. Females lay four to six eggs of ping-pong-ball size and leave for other territory: reptiles do not raise their young. When newly hatched, the tortoises are the size of silver dollars, and are miniatures of their parents, complete with yellowish brown shells intricately marked with tiny scutes, or horned plates. Since their shells remain soft for the first few years, the young are tasty appetizers for predators of all kinds, from badger to raven to human.

Tortoises live from seventy-five to one hundred years of age and begin to mate when they are fifteen years old. The bottom of the male's shell, the plastron, is slightly concave so that he may fit on top of the female's carapace.

The tortoise is an indicator species of the California desert, signaling the health or disease of an entire ecosystem. Just thirty years ago, motorists could often see tortoises throughout the California desert. Now, no longer—they are endangered. The greatest cause of their demise is the behavior of unthinking human beings. People collect them as pets, and in captivity they may die from respiratory disease. ORVs run over them and crush their homes. Tame tortoises released into the wild bring new diseases to which the desert

Through adolescence, which lasts until they are fifteen to twenty years old, tortoises have a wanderlust which puts them at risk for further predation. After they have traveled widely over the desert, an instinct that distributes the species over the landscape, they settle down in one place, build a deep burrow, and do not wander more than a quarter mile for the rest of their adult lives. From then on, 95 percent of their time is spent in their subterranean homes.

In Death Valley, winter temperatures can vary up to 40 degrees from day to night, too extreme a temperature range for an ectotherm, or cold-blooded animal. This means that tortoises must vary their environment, metabolic rate, and activity levels to survive. Although they can cope with temperatures as high as 128 degrees, too much unrelenting radiation can cook tortoises in the shell. During summer estivation, a temporary hibernation, they lower their metabolic rate and slow their heartbeat down to four beats a minute, thus reducing the amount of effort it takes to keep cool.

tortoise has no immunity. Vandals shoot or deliberately run over them. Even well-meaning humans who pick them up too quickly from the road surface in order to save their lives may cause them to urinate, and lose precious moisture. Since tortoises glean most of their fluids from the food they eat, any loss of moisture can kill them. Biologists assert that the only appropriate time to pick up a wild tortoise is to remove him from the road, but do so slowly and place him gently in the shade.

There is, however, great hope for the desert tortoise under the California Desert Protection Act. A number of the less-traveled new wilderness areas are home to healthy tortoise populations whose genes may successfully revitalize dying populations elsewhere. The military has also instituted extensive tortoise protection zones on weapons testing sites.

In the early morning and late afternoon I watch for a tortoise to emerge from its half-moon-shaped burrow to feed on tender new shoots or succulent cactus. It may be down as deep as thirty feet. I have a very long wait.

STILL WILD, ALWAYS WILD

At the top of Eureka Valley lie
the rugged Sylvania Mountains.

To understand a desert, it is necessary to know its edge, how it begins and ends. I'm in search of the edge of the California desert. As the first snow-covered domes of the southern Sierra loom in the distance, I have contradictory feelings. I have just traveled westward from Death Valley, over the Inyo Mountains, and dropped into the Panamint Valley. Within the hour I will leap up the Sierra Frontal fault into deep, snowy mountains—from 80-degree dry heat to bone-numbing cold in just a few miles.

There are seven new wilderness areas within these rugged, transitional mountains: the Kiavah, at 88,290 acres, is a major migration route for animals, while Chimney Peak's 13,700 acres protect endangered vegetation such as the cactus *Sclerocactus polyancistrus*. The Bright Star Wilderness is 9,520 acres of canyon country cactus gardens. The Sacatar Trail Wilderness blends the gentle terrain of the Kern Plateau with the extremely rugged high Sierra, while the Domeland Wilderness melds granite dome country with the desert foothills of the southern Sierra.

Although my return home is imminent, there are two wilderness areas I wish to explore: The Owens Peak Wilderness, 74,640 acres which soar to more than 8,400 feet in the space of twenty miles from the desert floor, and the Domeland Wilderness, 36,300 acres of Yosemite-like topography which is adjacent to the Sequoia National Forest Wilderness.

I drive over Walker Pass and the first line of foothills through a magnificent Joshua tree forest. Turning off on the road which will take me up between the Domeland and Owens Peak, I spy a slim dirt track shooting precariously up a two-thousand-foot mountain wall. "Sure am glad I don't have to go up that one," I think to myself. "Must be some crazy miner's road."

Twenty minutes later, as the nose of my truck tilts skyward up Canebreak Road and I shift nervously

Short Canyon on the fault escarpment side of the southern Sierra Nevada Mountains contains 280 species of blooming plants, such as sage.

From Desert to Mountain in One Leap

THE DOMELAND WILDERNESS

into first, I realize that this is that crazy road. Six miles up the sharp escarpment, deep sand traps coincide with hairpin curves. To negotiate them, I must accelerate at the exact instant caution tells me to slow down.

To keep myself from utter fright, I direct my mind to the more cheerful signs of the high Sierra: the blue flash of scrub jay and mountain bluebird, the lovely song of an Audubon's warbler, and the loud *rat-tat-tat-tat* of a woodland woodpecker. At 5,200 feet, I am welcomed by an open, sunny wood full of a long-needled Jeffrey pine, graceful trees with a wide crown.

No sooner am I relieved of cliff-hanging views of 2,000-foot drop-offs than snow appears mounded over the dark-shadowed road curves. I am still rising. On a 6,400-foot pass, I am so entranced by a landscape of huge white granite domes that I decide to pull over and sleep here inside my pickup. The wind whips up, and the temperature drops from 40 to 12 degrees by the time I go to sleep with all my clothing and a space blanket piled on top of my sleeping bag.

Due west, the next morning, I begin a gorgeous hike down Long Valley, a series of escarpments which drop down to the South Fork of the Kern River through country that looks like Yosemite National Park. The Kern is a very unusual river for the Sierra, where rivers usually flow west or east. The Kern flows south, along a major fault line, linking together many prehistoric village and rock art sites.

Returning to my truck, I explore the backside of the Chimney Peak Wilderness, then attempt to return to civilization, such as it is, in Inyokern.

Rather than frightening myself again on Canebreak Road, I take a paved road down Nine Mile Canyon. Dropping rapidly, five thousand feet down the steep Sierra Frontal escarpment, down vertical mountainsides the size of Kansas, I decide that this is one of the most spectacular roads in the United States. However, my brakes begin to stink, and I park on an 18-degree slope, putting huge stones in front of all four tires while the wheels cool. Afraid for my life and my pocketbook (I had already handed over a large hunk of cash at the garage in Inyokern last fall), I try to relax by dangling my feet down over vertiginous mountain slopes solid with wildflowers. Two hours and three plant guides later, I feel downright blissful.

After another two hours, having made it down the steep mountain escarpment, I sleep in Short Canyon on the east side of the Owens Peak Wilderness, where canyons shoot from the desert

Chrysopsis turns entire mountainsides bright yellow in the Owens Peak Wilderness Area.

floor straight up through four ecosystems with dizzying speed. This vertical landscape creates one of the richest, densest plant speciations in North America. Mary Ann Henry, the self-made botanist who has worked for fifty years to save such areas as Eureka Dunes and Owens Peak, has helped identify over 280 species of flowers in Short Canyon alone. She is standing with a group of flower enthusiasts who are dissecting a bloom when I, a complete stranger, walk up. The plant enthusiasts eye me curiously: I have not signed up for this spring tour up Short Canyon sponsored by the Maturango Museum in Ridgecrest. I had not planned to come, but here I am.

"Which primrose is that?" I ask, totally forgetting a proper greeting. People look slightly annoyed. Mary Ann spies a battered green book under my arm.

"Jaeger!" she cries in delight, referring to the desert flower–lover's bible. Instantly I am in the inner sanctum of the group, examining the internal parts of the bloom through a hand lens attached to somebody else's neck.

We mosey on up the trail exclaiming over the tiny yellow umbels of *Descurania*, the violets of gilia and lupine, the blue pollen of phlox, the papery cream cups, the weird stems of *Eriogonum nudum*, and one steep arroyo filled with the rare, endemic, Charlotte's phacelia. The more I delve into the minutia of flower taxonomy, the more I find myself living each moment fully.

Ah, the converts to natural history. I have found them from Alaska to Mexico, from alpine peak to desert floor, from wetlands to arid lands. Even the octogenarians, of which there are many, remain youthful, always imaginative, always curious, and always welcoming. They have the joy of a people who are infinitely fascinated with and deeply awed by every phenomenon around them. No expensive, consumptive lifestyles here—just wear a smile and a hand lens.

The northwestern Mojave ends dramatically in the Sierra Frontal fault with mountains that sweep up six thousand feet in a matter of miles.

Leaving Liquid Time

From Short Canyon, I drive northwest toward home. On my way up Walker Pass, my head is busy: "gotta get gas, gotta get supper, gotta fill my water bottles, gotta check the oil, gotta make it home in time to teach eighty adolescents about Puget Sound water quality. . . ." At the summit, I stop the truck and get out.

Gazing back at the vast desert floor exhaling gold in the last rays of sun, I feel estranged. How quickly I had chopped time into fragments.

I attempt to glue time back together, but find myself caught in yet another frantic notion: it is an endless effort to protect these last wilderness lands, to educate people, to enchant each and every child . . . letters to write . . . classrooms to visit . . . speeches to make.

I shake myself and try again. Where is desert time when I need it? I humbly ask the desert to come home to me. A lump rises in my throat. Far away, I imagine myself climbing up out of a subterranean home two thousand years ago to observe the turn of the silent constellations. The chance to flow through layers of time is granted to each of us who will give the desert a keen eye and quiet mind.

FROM DESERT TO MOUNTAIN IN ONE LEAP   **129**

BIBLIOGRAPHY

Balls, Edward K. *Early Uses of California Plants*, 1962, University of California Press, Berkeley, CA.

Bean, Lowell John, and Lisa J. Bourgeault. *The Cahuilla*, 1989, Chelsea House, New York, NY.

Benson, Lyman, and Robert A. Darrow. *Trees and Shrubs of the Southwestern Deserts,* revised third edition, 1981, University of Arizona Press, Tucson, AZ.

Bowers, Janice Emily. *Seasons of the Wind,* 1986, Northland Press, Flagstaff, AZ.

Bratton, Susan Power. "Sleeping with Lions, the Wild and the Holy," *Orion*, Summer 1991.

Brown, G. W., Jr. *Desert Biology: Special Topics on the Physical and Biological Aspects of Arid Regions, Volume I*, 1968, Harcourt Brace, New York, NY.

Hildebrand, Alan R., and William V. Boynton. "Cretaceous Ground Zero," *Natural History*, June 1991.

Holdren, J. P., and P. R. Ehrlich. "Human Population and the Global Environment," *American Science,* vol. 62, 1974.

Holmgren, Virginia C. *Owls in Folklore and Natural History*, 1988, Capra Press, Santa Barbara, CA.

Jaeger, Edmund C. *The California Deserts,* fourth edition, 1965, Stanford University Press, Stanford, CA.

Jaeger, Edmund C. *Desert Wild Flowers,* revised edition, 1969, Stanford University Press, Stanford, CA.

Jaeger, Edmund C. *Desert Wildlife,* revised edition, 1961, Stanford University Press, Stanford, CA.

Laird, Carobeth. *The Chemehuevis,* first edition, 1976, Malki Museum Press, Banning, CA.

Larson, Peggy. *A Sierra Club Naturalist's Guide: The Deserts of the Southwest,* 1977, Sierra Club Books, San Francisco, CA.

MacMahon, James A. *Deserts,* 1985, Alfred A. Knopf, New York, NY

Nabhan, Gary. "The Parable of the Poppy and the Bee," *Nature Conservancy*, March-April 1996.

Powell, Jerry A., and Charles L. Hogue. *California Insects,* 1979, University of California Press, Berkeley, CA

Schaffer, Vincent J., and John A. Day. *The Peterson Field Guide to the Atmosphere*, 1981, Houghton Mifflin, Boston, MA.

Sharp, Robert P. *A Field Guide to Southern California,* third edition, 1994, Kendall/Hunt Publishing, Dubuque, IA.

Sharp, Robert P., and Allen F. Glazner. *Geology Underfoot in Southern California,* 1993, Mountain Press, Missoula, MT.

The Sierra Club, *Decision for the Desert: The California Desert Protection Act*, 1989, The California Desert Protection League, San Francisco, CA .

Handbook of North American Indians, vols. 5, 6, and 8, 1978, Smithsonian Institute, Washington DC.

Snorf, John Sherwood, as told to Dorothy Snorf. *Early Days at Hart*, 1991, Tales of the Mojave Road Publishing, Essex, CA.

Stebbins, Robert A. *Field Guide to Western Reptiles*, 1966, Houghton Mifflin, New York, NY.

Storer, Tracy I., and Robert L. Usinger. *Sierra Nevada Natural History*, 1963, University of California Press, Berkeley, CA.

Strong, William Duncan. *Aboriginal Society in Southern California*, 1987, Malki Museum Press, Morongo Indian Reservation, Banning, CA.

Vitousek, P. M., P. R. Ehrlich, A. H. Ehrlich, and P. M. Matson. "Human Appropriation of the Products of Photosynthesis," *Biological Science*, 36 (6); 1986.

Williamson, Lt. R. S. *Explorations in California for Railroad Routes to Connect with the Routes Near the 35th and 32nd Parallels of the North Latitude,* 1853, War Department of the United States, Corp of Engineers, Washington DC.

Wilson, E. O. "Biological Diversity as a Scientific and Ethical Issue," Joint Meeting of Royal Society and American Philosophical Society, vol. 1, 1987.

Wilson, E. O., editor, and Frances M. Peter. *Biodiversity*, 1988, National Academy Press, Washington DC.

Zwinger, Ann. *These Mysterious Lands*, 1989, E. P. Dutton, New York, NY.

ACKNOWLEDGMENTS

This text represents the collective knowledge of many, dedicated volunteers and professionals alike. In addition to the thousands of individual citizens who wrote their letters and spoke with their congressional representatives, I want to thank Elden Hughes, Mary Ann Henry, Jim Dodson, Nick Erwin, and John Holstadt of the Sierra Club. Eddie and Jim Harmon of Ocotillo, and Marie Wright, Jim and Grace Rickard, Manfred Knaack, and geologist-ranger Fred Jee of Anza-Borrego taught me to think in Sonoran.

I am grateful for Don and Leanne Simons of El Centro and the many dedicated BLM rangers who know and protect the land, all the while scraping up drunken bodies off the Algodones Dunes on holidays.

Stew Churchwell, BLM volunteer in the Chuckwallas, and Rangers Gloria Gillette and Elizabeth Van Zadt of Joshua Tree were full of great ideas.

Thom Thompson and Mark Faull, de facto directors-researchers-protectors of Mitchell Caverns and Red Rock Canyon State Parks, work many hours beyond their paid allotment, and were enthusiastic teachers.

National Park Service Rangers Charlie Callagan and Kevin Emmerich and Librarian Blaire Johnson of Death Valley helped a great deal, while Ranger Allen Van Valkenburg's plant lore delighted me.

David Ganger, petroglyph tour leader, and Edna Laytart of the Maturango Museum in Ridgecrest were so knowledgeable and enthusiastic, I'd follow them anywhere.

Thanks to the good folk of Tehabi Books who put up with text fragments flying in from obscure desert regions, and my friends and cocreators—Ann Zwinger, Jeff Garton, Ann Davenport, Susan Scott, Susan Farbor, and Gary Nabhan—who patiently listened to me moan and groan, and then reminded me of the transcendant nature of the desert.— *SUSAN ZWINGER*, PUGET SOUND, WASHINGTON

* * *

I want to thank the many people who supplied me with information that made it easier for me to photograph the many areas included in this book: Elden Hughes of the Sierra Club, Bob Reynolds of the San Bernardino County Museum, the BLM employees Tim Singer, Jim Dodson, and Don and Leanne Simmons, the Joshua Tree National Park employees Elizabeth Van Zandt and Gloria Gillette. And thanks to Jim and Eddie Harmon who provided me a cool meeting place out of the hot sun.

I enjoyed spending time in the desert with Susan Zwinger. Her barbecued chicken dinners were a real treat. And as always, a special thanks to my wife, Melissa, for running the office while I was out in the field.—*JEFF GARTON*, TUCSON, ARIZONA

INDEX

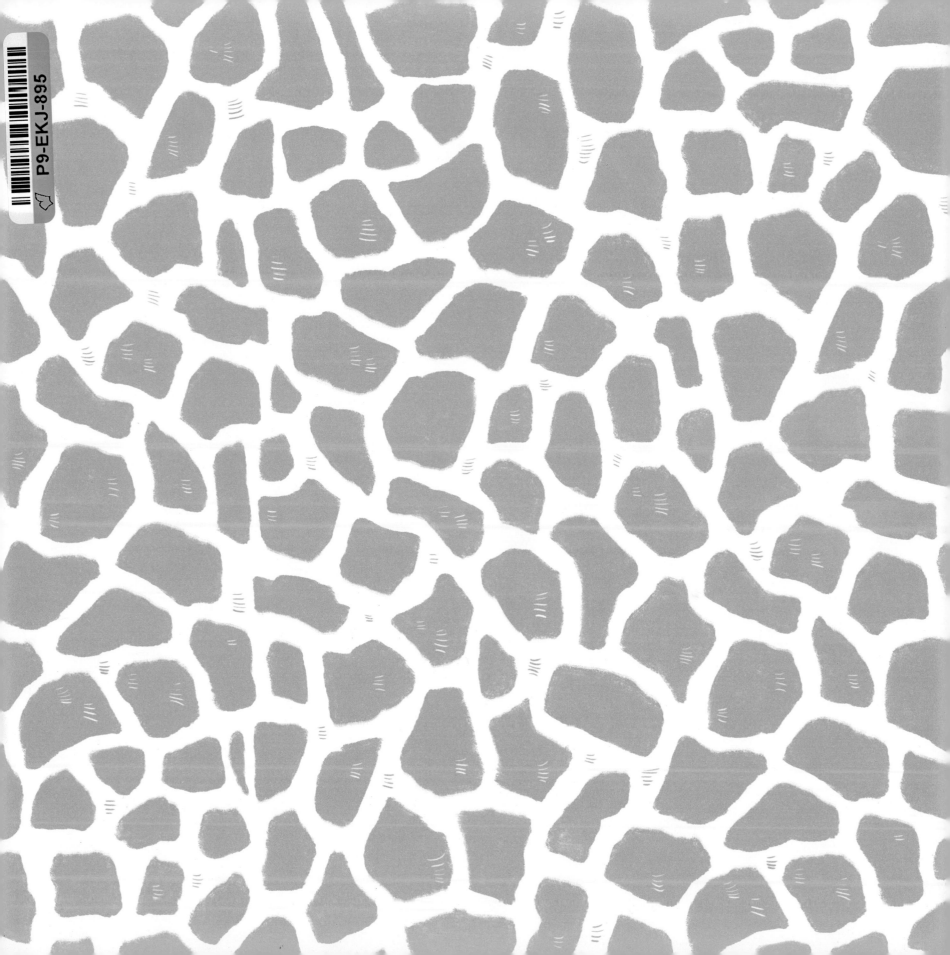

SECRETS
OF
ANIMAL
CAMOUFLAGE

Carron Brown

Illustrated by Wesley Robins

A DIVISION OF EDC PUBLISHING

Some animals are good at hiding because of their color or pattern. This is called camouflage.

If you look closely among the flowers and trees, on the seabed, and in the grasslands, you may be able to spot hidden animals.

Shine a flashlight behind the page, or hold it up to the light to reveal the animals hiding in their habitats. Discover a world of great surprises.

These busy bees are collecting pollen from the yellow and white flowers. But they need to be careful.

Who is watching them?

Two whitebanded crab spiders
are waiting to pounce!
The spiders change color
to match the yellow and
white flowers, so the bees
don't notice them.

Scuttle!

A brightly colored trogon
is perched in a tree. He is
hungry and on the lookout
for insects to eat.

Can you spot any?

Rustle!

A long, leggy walking stick is
balancing on the branch.
It looks just like a twig!
The walking stick stays still
all day. It moves at night,
when most birds are asleep.

Shhh! Something has disturbed this family of axis deer.

Is something prowling through the grass?

It's a fierce Bengal tiger!
Her orange coat with long
stripes makes her hard to spot
in the tall golden grass.

Growl!

A nimble fox
squirrel has scurried
up this tree. He is
searching for the hollow
in the trunk, where he
will make a nest.

Can you see what is
covering it?

Screech!

It's a screech owl!
Her patterned feathers
match the colors of the
tree bark. The owl can
stay very still—it makes
it difficult to see her.

A white-tailed deer
is going deeper into
the forest to look
for food.

What is she leaving
behind?

Shhhh!

It's her baby—a fawn—with a red-brown coat and white spots. The color of its coat helps to hide it in the red-brown leaves. When the mother has found food, she will return to feed her fawn.

In the grassland,
a baby giraffe pulls
the leaves from a tree.

Who is eating the treetops?

Stretch!

The mother giraffe, that's who!
She lengthens her long neck
to reach the topmost leaves.
The dark markings on her
light-colored coat help her
to hide among the leaves and
sunlit patches in the tree.

This little green lizard
is frightened. An owl is staring
at it from behind the leaves.

Can you see the owl's eyes?

It's OK! They're not really an owl's eyes—just two large spots on an owl butterfly's wings.

Flutter!

By disguising itself, the butterfly protects itself from the lizard because lizards are scared of owls.

What beautiful orchid flowers!

Guess what? One of them is really an insect. Can you spot it?

The orchid mantis looks just like a flower. It is pink and white, and four of its six legs are shaped like petals. This clever disguise helps to keep it safe.

Snap!

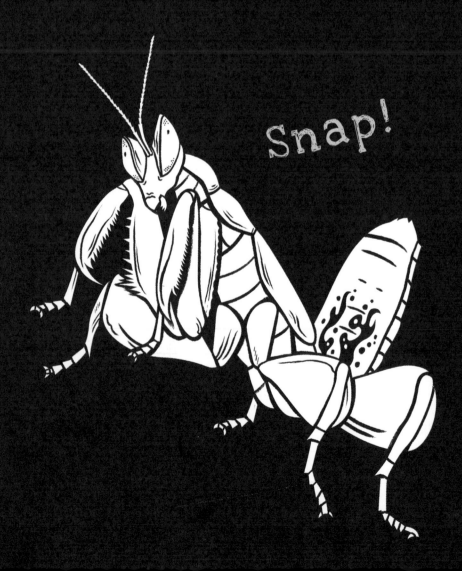

It's easy to mistake a Malayan leaf frog for fallen leaves.

How many frogs can you see?

There are two!

These horned frogs have skin
that is folded to look like a leaf.
It's the perfect disguise for
hiding on the forest floor.

Croak!

Something wants
to trap this fly.

Can you see
what it is?

Slurp!

This creeping green chameleon is the same color as the leaves. It has a long, sticky tongue that flicks out to catch insects.

A herd of zebras race
across the African plain.
A lion watches them.

Do you know why they all
run together?

Trot!

The zebras run together in a group to trick the lion. It cannot see only one zebra among so many stripes, so it leaves the herd alone.

On a cold, snowy day, three furry lemmings are searching for food.

Who is watching them?

Bark!

It's an Arctic fox! Its long fur grows
thick and white in winter to keep it
warm and hide it in the snow.
In summer, its coat is thin
and brown.

A very strange creature
with eight legs is resting
on the sandy seabed.

Can you see what
it is?

Slither!

It's a blue-ringed octopus. It can change
the color of its skin to match the
seabed. When it is frightened, blue rings
flash on its body! The flashes tell other
animals that it is poisonous.

A group of tiny pygmy seahorses swim
past a tangle of pink coral.

How many can you see?

Six!

The seahorses look just
like the coral they live on.
To stop themselves floating away,
they grip the coral with their
strong, curled tails.

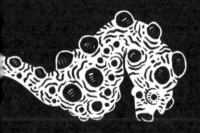

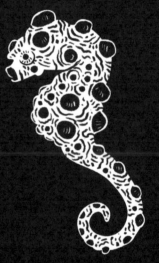

Bubble!

A small hermit crab scuttles across the sand. It has no shell of its own, but has borrowed an empty seashell to live in.

Who is looking at the crab?

Flap!

A beady-eyed flatfish, called a
plaice, has buried itself in the
sand. First it changed color to
match the seabed. Then it shook
its fins to throw sand over its body.

People can use camouflage too.
Wearing clothes patterned in green,
gray and brown is a great disguise
for nature watchers.

Stay quiet, still and hidden, and you
might see animals up close.

There's more...

Look closely in the long grass, flowers, trees, at snowy lands and into the ocean to spot animals hiding in their homes all over the world.

Flower spiders The whitebanded crab spiders that hide in white and yellow flowers live in North America. They eat the bees, flies and wasps that visit the flowers.

Lost in twigs Walking sticks are from India, but some escaped pet walking sticks live hidden in bushes and trees in Europe, Africa and the USA.

Stripes in grass Bengal tigers hunt for animals to eat in the grasslands of India, Nepal, Bhutan and Bangladesh.

Brown and gray Eastern screech owls nest in trees in the USA, Canada and Mexico. Their feathers are the color of tree bark, but they have large yellow eyes.

Hard to spot White-tailed deer are from North America, but people have taken them to live in other places around the world.

Tall trunks Giraffes live in the dry grasslands of Africa. The adults are so tall that they reach the treetops and look like parts of the tree with dark and light patches.

Eye spots Owl butterflies fly in the rain forests of South America. They sip the sweet juices of fruit and flowers.

Snappy flower Orchid mantises perch on orchid flowers in Southeast Asia. They eat other insects that land on the flower.

Leafy disguise Malayan leaf frogs live in Malaysian rain forests. They look like fallen leaves on the ground.

Hidden in color Green chameleons come from North America and southern Europe. Their color and swaying motion make them look like leaves.

Safety in numbers Zebras roam the grasslands and woodlands of Africa. Because of their stripes, it is hard to see where one zebra starts and another ends.

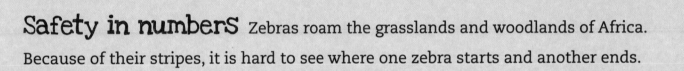

Summer coat Arctic foxes live in the cold north of Europe, Asia and North America. In summer, their fur changes to brown and is thin to keep them cool.

Warning colors Blue-ringed octopuses swim around the coasts of Australia and Japan. They change color to scare hunters—they have a nasty bite!

Perfect match Pygmy seahorses live on coral in the western Pacific Ocean. These small fish curl their tails around coral that is exactly the same color as them.

Color changer Plaice are fish that are found on the seabed in the seas around northern Europe. They change color to match sand or stone.

First American Edition 2016
Kane Miller, A Division of EDC Publishing

Copyright © 2016 Ivy Kids (an imprint of Ivy Press Ltd)

For information contact:
Kane Miller, A Division of EDC Publishing
PO Box 470663
Tulsa, OK 74147-0663
www.kanemiller.com
www.edcpub.com
www.usbornebooksandmore.com

Library of Congress Control Number: 2015954247

Printed in China

ISBN: 978-1-61067-466-9